STRAIGHT TO HEAVEN

Rev. T. G. Morrow

STRAIGHT
TO HEAVEN

*A Practical Guide
for Growing in Holiness*

SOPHIA INSTITUTE PRESS
Manchester, New Hampshire

Sophia Institute Press
Box 5284, Manchester, NH 03108
1-800-888-9344
www.SophiaInstitute.com

Sophia Institute Press is a registered trademark of Sophia Institute.

paperback ISBN 978-1-64413-824-3

ebook ISBN 978-1-64413-825-0

Library of Congress Control Number: 2022949474

Author's Note

All Biblical quotes are from the RSV, Catholic
Edition, unless otherwise noted. The stories given
herein are true, but some of the incidentals have been
changed to protect the privacy of those involved.

CONTENTS

PART III
THE LIFE OF VIRTUE

STRAIGHT TO HEAVEN

INTRODUCTION

A YOUNG BOY once told his mother, "I don't want to go to Heaven."

"Why not?" she asked.

"Because I think it's boring," he responded.

She realized she had a major task to prove to him that Heaven was certainly not boring; in fact, it is the most exciting, delightful place we could ever imagine. She must have done a good job—he now goes all across the country to tell his conversion story to Catholic youth.

Why is it that so few people today strive for holiness? Why so few who even seek any religious involvement, any morality in their lives? I think a major reason is that they have been lulled to sleep about the most critical moment they will ever face: divine judgment. If more people kept in mind that they will surely die one day and meet the Lord—at which time their eternal destiny will be sealed—they might be more dedicated to preparing for that crucial day.

Add to this the all-important knowledge as to just what they can expect on that day, based on how they have lived, and we have powerful motivations to live the gospel. Alas, many believe nowadays that Heaven is boring, Hell is empty, and Purgatory is like a doctor's waiting-room. Not so, according to Christ and His Church. Far from it!

It does not matter what success we have had in this world: if we are rich, or famous, or have scores of wonderful friends. If, at the end of our lives, we don't make it to the Kingdom, all is wasted. Our Blessed Lord said as much: "For what will it profit a man, if he gains the whole world and forfeits his life? Or what shall a man give in return for his life?" (Matt. 16:26).

PART I

Motivations for Holiness

THE DELIGHT OF HEAVEN: THE DIVINE MARRIAGE

Sт. Augustine was born of a womanizing father but a devout mother, and in his early years he took after his father. He moved in with his mistress at the age of sixteen and lived with her for the next fourteen years. Meanwhile his mother, Monica, stormed Heaven for him. At the age of thirty-one he had a conversion. As he prepared for Baptism, he began to pray and do penance for his past life of sin. Eighteen months after his Baptism his mother died, happy to see his conversion. Three years later, Augustine was ordained a priest. Four years after that, he became a bishop. He became one of the most prolific writers the Church has ever known. In his autobiography, *Confessions*, he wrote beautifully of his conversion:

> Late have I loved you, O Beauty so ancient and so new.... I rushed headlong after these things of beauty which you have made.... They kept me far from you, those fair things which, were they not in you, would not exist at all.... You have sent forth fragrance, and I have drawn in my breath, and I pant for you. I have tasted you, and I hunger and thirst for you. You have touched me, and I have burned for your peace.[1]

---

[1] St. Augustine of Hippo, *The Confessions of St. Augustine*, trans. by John K. Ryan, New York: Image Books, 1960, book 10, chapter 27. p. 220. This quote has been adapted slightly.

Augustine tasted the illicit delights of this world and was perceptive enough to realize they didn't satisfy. After just a taste of Heaven, experienced through prayer and fasting, he realized that all the beauty, all the joys of this world are just a whisper of the beauty and joy to be found in God, both in this life and in the life to come. That is the first task of every Christian, of every person: to discover the unfathomable glory of being united with God, now and forever. But first we must find motivation in the goal God has given us, namely, Heaven.

THE BASICS

Our Blessed Lord refers to Heaven, using several different terms, about 170 times in the Gospels. He uses the terms *Heaven, Kingdom of Heaven, Kingdom of God, life,* and *eternal life* to describe this place of eternal reward. He often speaks of the Kingdom by comparing it to things we are familiar with on earth:

> The kingdom of heaven is like treasure hidden in a field, which a man found and covered up; then in his joy he goes and sells all that he has and buys that field. Again, the kingdom of heaven is like a merchant in search of fine pearls, who, on finding one pearl of great value, went and sold all that he had and bought it. (Matt. 13:44–46)

Twice he speaks of the Kingdom as being like a wedding feast (Matt. 22:1–14; 25:1–13), as does the author of the book of Revelation (Rev. 19:7–9). Thus, our Lord clearly speaks of the Kingdom of Heaven as something very valuable, worth selling all you have to possess, as a feast celebrating a commitment of love, and as a rich reward for whatever sacrifice we make here on earth.

St. Paul speaks of Heaven in glowing terms: "No eye has seen, nor ear heard, nor the heart of man conceived, what God has prepared for those who love him" (1 Cor. 2:9). It is beyond anything we can imagine.

Will everyone be at the same level in Heaven, or will some receive a greater reward than others? We find the answer in Church teaching: "[The souls of those who enter Heaven] clearly behold the triune God as he is, yet one person more perfectly than another according to the difference of their merits."[2] This is based on the words of our Lord: "The Son of man ... will reward each one according to his conduct," (Matt. 16:27)[3] and the words of St. Paul: "Each shall receive his wages according to his labor" (1 Cor. 3:8; see also 2 Cor. 9:6).

Many of the saints wrote of the tremendous joy and happiness that awaits those who are worthy of Heaven: To paraphrase St. Augustine, what must be the amazing joy of those in Heaven, seeing how much beauty, how many delights, and what great blessings we enjoy on earth? St. Teresa of Ávila remarked, "Our life lasts only a couple of hours. Our reward is boundless."[4] St. Thérèse of Lisieux said,

I have formed such a lofty idea of heaven that, at times, I wonder what God will do at my death to surprise me. My hope is so great, it is such a subject of joy to me, not by feeling but by faith, that to satisfy me fully something will be necessary which is beyond all human conception.[5]

St. Catherine of Siena wrote, "The indescribable sweetness of this perfect union cannot be told by tongue, which is but a finite thing." And, from St. John of the Cross:

---

[2] Council of Florence, Session 6, July 6, 1439, found at https://www.ewtn.com/catholicism/library/ecumenical-council-of-florence-1438-1445-1461.

[3] Author's translation.

[4] St. Teresa of Ávila, *The Way of Perfection*, trans. by E. Allison Peers, New York: Image Books, 1964, chapter 2, n. 7, p. 43.

[5] St. Thérèse to Mother Agnes, found in *St. Thérèse of Lisieux, St. Thérèse of Lisieux: Her Last Conversations*, trans. by John Clarke, Washington, DC: ICS Publications, 1977, p. 29.

Were (the soul) to have but a foreglimpse of the height and beauty of God, she would not only desire death in order to see him now forever, as she here desires, but she would very gladly undergo a thousand singularly bitter deaths to see Him only for a moment; and having seen Him, she would ask to suffer just as many more that she might see Him for another moment.[6]

What is heaven like? Do we have any clues, more than just a place with many clouds, and gold streets? It is primarily a relationship. But what sort of a relationship?

THE DIVINE MARRIAGE

St. Gregory the Great said heaven would be like a marriage: "The husband of every Christian soul is God; for she is joined to Him by faith."[7] St. John of the Cross wrote along the same line:

One does not reach this garden of full transformation which is the joy, delight and glory of spiritual marriage, without first passing through the spiritual espousal and the loyal and mutual love of betrothed persons. For, after the soul has been for some time the betrothed of the Son of God in gentle and complete love, God calls her and places her in His flowering garden to consummate this most joyful state of marriage with Him.... Yet in this life this union cannot be perfect, although it is beyond words and thought.[8]

---

[6] St. John of the Cross, *The Spiritual Canticle*, found in *The Collected Works of St. John of the Cross*, trans. by Kieran Kavanaugh, O.C.D. and Otilio Rodriguez, O.C.D., Washington, DC: ICS Publications, 1979, p. 450.

[7] St. Gregory the Great, *The Supper of God and the Soul*, found in *The Sunday Sermons of the Great Fathers*, Vol. III, ed. and trans. by M. F. Toal, San Francisco: Ignatius Press, p. 186.

[8] St. John of the Cross, *The Spiritual Canticle*, found in *The Collected Works of St. John of the Cross*, p. 497.

Thus, according to St. John, the "spiritual marriage" begins here on earth, not just in the Kingdom.

In 1572, the Lord spoke to St. Teresa of Ávila as follows: "You will be my bride from today on. Until now you have not merited this; from now on, not only will you look after my honor as [that of] your Creator, King and God, but ... as my true bride."[9]

Others, including Sts. Margaret of Cortona, Catherine of Siena, Lawrence Justinian, John of God, and John Vianney received wedding rings from the Lord.[10] When St. Margaret Mary Alacoque suffered great temptations against her vocation to be a nun, Jesus appeared to her one day after Communion and showed her that He was "the most beautiful, the wealthiest, the most powerful, the most perfect and the most accomplished among all lovers."[11] He told her He had chosen her to be His spouse. After this she hesitated no more to enter the convent!

There are several biblical passages that support this marriage-with-God theme. In Ezekiel 16, the Lord addresses His people, Jerusalem, as His unfaithful spouse with whom He later restores His covenant. In Isaiah 62:4–5, we read:

> You shall no more be termed Forsaken,
> and your land shall no more be termed Desolate;
> but you shall be called My delight is in her,
> and your land Married;
> for the LORD delights in you,
> and your land shall be married.

---

[9] St. Teresa of Ávila, *Spiritual Testimonies*, found in *The Collected Works of St. Teresa of Ávila*, vol. I, trans. by Kieran Kavanaugh, O.C.D. and Otilio Rodriguez, O.C.D., Washington, D.C.: ICS Publications, 1976, p. 336.

[10] Abbé Francis Trochu, *The Curé d'Ars: St. Jean-Marie Baptiste Vianney*, trans. by Dom Ernest Graf, Rockford, IL: TAN Books, 1977, p. 545.

[11] St. Margaret Mary Alacoque, *The Autobiography of Saint Margaret Mary*, Rockford, IL: TAN Books, 1986 p. 40.

> For as a young man marries a virgin,
>> so shall your sons marry you,
> and as the bridegroom rejoices over the bride,
>> so shall your God rejoice over you.[12]

In Isaiah 54:5, we find, "Your Maker is your husband, the LORD of hosts is his name." In Revelation 19:7, there is rejoicing because "the marriage of the Lamb [Jesus] has come, and his Bride has made herself ready." Hosea 1 and 2 contain God's complaint against Israel: "The land commits great harlotry by forsaking the LORD" (Hos. 1:2); God leads her back to Him and says after her return, "And I will betroth you to me for ever; I will betroth you to me in righteousness and in justice, in steadfast love, and in mercy. I will betroth you to me in faithfulness; and you shall know the LORD" (Hos. 2:19–20).

The implications of this heavenly marriage are important. If we are to be in a kind of marriage with God, Who is so holy, we must be holy ourselves. A marriage in which one party loves at an intensely high level and the other loves feebly simply won't do. In order for us to be in this eternal marriage, we must somehow be energized or super-charged to love God at least at a quasi-reciprocal level. We must love God with *His* power, in other words, with *His* Spirit.

How much of the Holy Spirit do we need to be in this marriage? It doesn't take a rocket scientist to know it takes 100 percent, that is, we must be filled to capacity. The more the Holy Spirit dwells within us, the more we are ready for this marriage.

If you had the spirit of Mozart, you could write great music. If you had the spirit of Shakespeare, you could write great plays. But, if you have the Spirit of God, you can love at a quasi-divine level.

---

[12] *New American Bible*, New York: Catholic Book Publishing Co., 1991.

This need for profound holiness is fully supported elsewhere in Sacred Scripture. In Luke 10:27, we are told that the condition for entering eternal life is to "love the Lord your God with all your heart, and with all your soul, and with all your strength, and with all your mind; and your neighbor as yourself."

There is other biblical evidence for the need to be holy. Jesus said in Matthew 5:48: "You, therefore, must be perfect, as your heavenly Father is perfect." In Leviticus 19:2, we read, "Be holy; for I the LORD your God am holy" (see also Lev. 11:45; 20:7). In addition, we read in Ephesians 1:4, "He chose us in him before the foundation of the world, that we should be holy and blameless before him" (see also Eph. 5:27, 1 Pet. 1:15–16; 2:5).

Vatican II speaks of this call to holiness:

> Thus it is evident to everyone, that all the faithful of Christ of whatever rank or status, are called to the fullness of the Christian life and to the perfection of charity; by this holiness as such a more human manner of living is promoted in this earthly society.[13]

The Lord appeared to St. Margaret Mary at one point and told her, "Learn that I am a Holy Master and One that teaches holiness. I am pure and cannot endure the slightest stain."[14] Thus, it should be clear: to live in this heavenly marriage with God, we must be *very* holy.

How foolish we would be to underestimate the holiness we must arrive at to be worthy of the Kingdom. Living in the state of grace is enough to be saved, that is, to be worthy of Purgatory. However,

---

[13] Vatican II, *Lumen Gentium* (Constitution on the Church), November 21, 1964, n. 40, found at https://www.ewtn.com/catholicism/library/dogmatic-constitution-on-the-church-1513.

[14] St. Margaret Mary Alacoque, *The Autobiography of Saint Margaret Mary*, p. 64.

to be worthy of entering the Kingdom, we must surrender all. For those who do well but do not give their all in this life, Purgatory awaits. And, as we shall see, Purgatory is not a pleasant prospect.

HARD BUT SWEET

Loving God at that level is no easy task. Nor is loving our neighbor as ourselves. Jesus told us it would be hard: "Enter by the narrow gate; for the gate is wide and the way is easy, that leads to [eternal] destruction, and those who enter by it are many. For the gate is narrow and the way is hard, that leads to [eternal] life, and those who find it are few" (Matt. 7:13–14). Elsewhere He said, "[Whoever] would come after me, let him deny himself and take up his cross and follow me" (Mark 8:34). Clearly, it will be a difficult path to come to this level of love.

However, Jesus did promise He would sweeten the journey: "Come to me, all who labor and are heavy laden, and I will give you rest. Take my yoke upon you, and learn from me; for I am gentle and lowly in heart, and you will find rest for your souls. For my yoke is easy [or gentle], and my burden is light" (Matt. 11:28–30).

A PLAN

If we were to die tomorrow and had to admit to the Lord, "I confess, I hadn't come to love You with all my heart, soul, and mind," He would, we might speculate, be very understanding. But, if we died tomorrow and had to admit that we not only had not come to this level of love, but we had had no *plan* as to how to get there, we should anticipate some great displeasure on His part. We *need* a plan. That plan is the subject of this book.

A ROMANTIC VIEW OF HEAVEN

St. John of the Cross wrote of the beauty of the encounter with God:

Since the virtues of the bride are perfect she enjoys habitual peace in the visits of her Beloved. She sometimes has a sublime enjoyment of their sweetness and fragrance when her Beloved touches these virtues, just as a man enjoys the sweetness and beauty of flowers and lilies when they have blossomed, and he must handle them. The soul feels that the Beloved is within her as in His own bed. She offers herself together with her virtues, which is the greatest service she can render Him. Thus, one of the most remarkable delights she receives in her interior communion with God comes from this gift of herself to her beloved.[15]

We should think often of the utter delight of Heaven. Imagine being married to the most desirable member of the opposite sex you could ever conceive of.[16]A chaste embrace with the God Who created in His own image the beauties we so desire on earth, and Who has called us to be His spouse, is an image of Heaven which is a mere whisper of the actual delight and glory of Heaven. By using this sort of healthy "fantasy," we can inspire ourselves to strive harder in prayer and other spiritual activities.

---

[15] St. John of the Cross, *The Spiritual Canticle*, found in *The Collected Works of St. John of the Cross*, pp. 474, 475.

[16] This takes more imagination for men than for women, to be sure. However, the *Catechism of the Catholic Church* teaches, "We ought therefore to recall that God transcends the human distinction between the sexes. He is neither man nor woman: he is God" (CCC 239). We call Him by male names and pronouns because He has a male role in relationship to us (provider, pursuer, etc.). Thus, the soul is always feminine in spiritual writing (as above). Men who have difficulty imagining this embrace should realize that both men and women are created in the image and likeness of God. When a man sees the beauty of a woman, body and soul, he sees a reflection of the beauty of God.

We might pray thus:

O God, I have always dreamed of a lover like You: beautiful to the core beyond telling, kind, charming, alluring, fascinating, unfathomable, and faithful. You are so warmly inviting, yet You graciously and firmly correct my selfishness. O that You might always call me to that intimate eucharistic Communion with You, body and soul even in my imperfect but sincere love, as a sign and promise of the ecstatic intimacy to which You call me in the eternal marriage of Your Kingdom; an intimacy which married couples on earth could never dream of.

St. John of the Cross provided this rather amazing insight into the humility of God in Heaven:

The tenderness and truth of love by which the immense Father favors and exalts this humble and loving soul reaches such a degree — O wonderful thing, worthy of all our aim and admiration! — the Father Himself becomes subject to her for her exaltation, as though He were her servant and she His Lord. And He is as solicitous in favoring her as He would be if He were her slave and she His God. So profound is the humility and sweetness of God![17]

No doubt for some this romantic approach to God might seem strange or even uncomfortable. Yet, it is fully in accord with the Scriptures and with the writings of the saints. Hosea 1 and 2 and Ezekiel 16 are examples of how the prophets, as Pope Benedict XVI wrote, "described God's passion for His people, using boldly erotic

---

[17] St. John of the Cross, *The Spiritual Canticle*, found in *The Collected Works of St. John of the Cross*, p. 517.

images."[18] The Song of Songs and the *Spiritual Canticle* of St. John of the Cross are further expressions of this recurring theme of God as our passionate, intimate lover.

Ultimately, it is only union with this Beloved that will fulfill us completely as persons, and an imaginary chaste embrace of such a Lover is a noble fantasy, a powerful sign of that intimate union. And, it is more real than any earthly fantasy could ever be. Such an image should move us to pray and worship our God, that we might be worthy of this eternal, joyful, peaceful, divine marriage with this "Beauty so ancient and so new."

✠ ✠ ✠

The thought of Heaven should be on our minds constantly. There must never be a day where we forget the glory that awaits us if we strive for the holiness to which God invites us. We should contemplate this joyful reality several times — even scores of times — daily, that we might be ever aware of our purpose on this earth to become a worthy gift to live in that Kingdom of love forever.

---

[18] Pope Benedict XVI, encyclical *Deus Caritas Est*, 2005, as found at https://www.ewtn.com/catholicism/library/deus-caritas-est-3354 n. 9.

2

THE REALITY OF HELL

In this age of pseudo-sophistication, the mention of Hell is considered much too harsh for polite company. I heard of one Catholic saying in public, "If there is a Hell, there's no one there." Alas, there is no evidence in Scripture, in the teaching of the Church, or in the writings of the saints to support such a statement. St. Josemaría Escrivá wrote, "There is a hell. A trite enough statement, you think. I will repeat it, then: there is a hell! Echo it, at the right moment, in the ears of one friend and another, and another."[19] The saints did not shy away from mentioning Hell.

Our Lord refers to Hell and its punishment fewer than thirty times in the Gospels as compared to about 170 references to Heaven. Thus, while His emphasis is certainly on the positive, He does not leave out the negative. He uses the terms *Hades* and *Gehenna*, both translated as *Hell*, but more often He speaks of fire, everlasting fire, or unquenchable fire.

If your foot causes you to sin, cut it off; it is better for you to enter life lame than with two feet to be thrown into hell. And if your eye causes you to sin, pluck it out; it is better for you to enter the kingdom of God with one eye than

[19] St. Josemaría Escrivá, *The Way, Furrow, The Forge*, New York: Scepter, 2001, n. 749, pp. 187, 188.

with two eyes to be thrown into hell, where their worm
does not die, and the fire is not quenched. (Mark 9:45–48)

Of course, our Lord is not literally suggesting that anyone should cut
off his hand or tear out his eye. He uses these comparisons simply
to indicate the terrible nature of Hell, and the sin which sends one
there. It seems He accomplished His goal very well, for the words
are truly frightening.

Does anyone go to Hell? There is, of course no way of knowing
who *does* go to Hell, but as we saw earlier, our Blessed Lord did say:

> Enter by the narrow gate; for the gate is wide and the way
> is easy, that leads to [eternal] destruction, and those who
> enter by it are many. For the gate is narrow and the way is
> hard, that leads to [eternal] life, and those who find it are
> few. (Matt. 7:13–14)

Jesus also said, "Many are called, but few are chosen" (Matt. 22:14).
Some people wonder if perhaps at some point in time Hell might
end and all the souls be released. This is not a new idea. Origen, a
theologian in the early Church, believed, as did some others, that
Hell would not last for all eternity. However, the Church condemned
this idea, declaring that the punishment of Hell would last for all
eternity (Fourth Lateran Council). This was no doubt based on the
use of the word *eternal* or *everlasting* in Scripture when describing
the punishment of Hell (see Matt. 25:41, 46; 2 Thess. 1:9).

Many people through the ages have had great difficulty in imagining that there is such a thing as Hell, in light of all the revelations
about God's goodness and mercy. The doctrine of Hell is truly a
mystery with which we must struggle, even after it has clearly been
spelled out to us, and yet the Church Doctors were all agreed on
their acceptance of this doctrine. St. Augustine wrote, "[Hell] is

not a matter of feeling, but a fact.... There is no way of waiving or weakening the words which the Lord has told us He will pronounce at the Last Judgment."[20] St. Bernard of Clairvaux urged us to go down into Hell now (by way of imagination) so that we don't end up there when we die. St. John Chrysostom said something similar: "What can be more grievous than hell? Yet nothing is more profitable than the fear of it."[21] St. Teresa of Ávila related the following:

I was at prayer one day when I suddenly found that, without knowing how, I had seemingly been put in Hell. I understood that the Lord wanted me to see the place the devils had prepared there for me and which I merited because of my sins.... I felt a fire in the soul that I don't know how I could describe. The bodily pains were so unbearable that, though I had suffered excruciating ones in this life, and according to what the doctors say, the worst that can be suffered on earth (for all my nerves were shrunken when I was paralyzed ...), these were nothing in comparison with what I experienced there. I saw furthermore that they would go on without end.... This, however, was nothing next to the soul's agonizing: a constriction, a suffocation, an affliction so keenly and deeply felt ... that I don't know how to word it strongly enough.[22]

[20] St. Augustine of Hippo, *The City of God*, 22, 23, from Fr. John Hardon, "Demonology," found at http://www.therealpresence.org/archives/Demonology/Demonology_002.htm.

[21] St. John Chrysostom, *Homilies on the Statutes*, homily 15, found in *Saint Chrysostom: On the Priesthood; Ascetic Treatises; Select Homilies and Letters; Homilies on the Statutes*, found in *Nicene and Post-Nicene Fathers*, vol. IX, ed. by Philip Schaff, Grand Rapids, MI: Wm. B. Eerdmans, found at http://www.ccel.org/ccel/schaff/npnf109.xix.xvii.html.

[22] St. Teresa of Ávila, *The Book of Her Life*, found in *The Collected Works of St. Teresa of Ávila*, vol. I, p. 213.

A concept that arose in the twelfth century speaks of two pains in Hell: the pain of loss, of not seeing God; and the pain of sense, a burning sensation. St. Catherine of Siena received this insight from the Lord, "They see themselves deprived of the vision of Me, which is such pain to them, that, were it possible, they would rather choose the fire, and the tortures and torments, and to see Me, than to be without the torments and not to see Me."[23] Thus, the pain of not seeing God is far more agonizing than the pain of sense.

St. Francis de Sales dedicated an entire chapter in his *Introduction to the Devout Life* to a reflection on Hell. An excerpt of that follows:

> Picture to yourself a dark city, reeking with the flames of sulphur and brimstone, inhabited by citizens who cannot get out.
>
> Even so the lost are plunged in their infernal abyss—suffering indescribable torture in every sense and every member; and that because having used their members and senses for sin, it is just that through them they should suffer now. Those eyes which delighted in impure vicious sights, now behold devils; the ears which took pleasure in unholy words, now are deafened with yells of despair....
>
> Beyond all these sufferings, there is one greater still, the privation and pain of loss of God's Glory, which is forever denied to their vision....
>
> Consider how insupportable the pains of Hell will be by reason of their eternal duration. If the irritating bite of an insect, or the restlessness of fever, makes an ordinary night seem so long and tedious, how terrible will the

---

[23] St. Catherine of Siena, *The Dialogue of St. Catherine of Siena*, trans. by Algar Thorold, Rockford, IL: 1974, TAN Books, p. 105.

endless night of eternity be, where nothing will be found save despair, blasphemy and fury![24]

FREEDOM AND LOVE

The mystery of Hell is wrapped up with our freedom and the justice of God. Although God is all-merciful, one who enters Hell has rejected God's mercy, and God does not overrule his choice. Consider this simple analogy. Let's say you come upon someone working on his computer, trying to solve a problem that you solved on your own computer the previous year. And, suppose you offer him some advice, explaining that you had the same problem a year ago, and it took you six months to solve it. "If you want," you explain, "I can help you get it fixed in about half an hour."

But, let's say he rejects your offer, saying, "Look, I don't need your help. I can fix it myself." You can't very well force him to accept your help. Thus, because he is too proud to accept your help, he is left to his problem, which he may *never* solve. You might say, as you leave, "If you change your mind, call me."

So it is with the Lord. He comes along and tells us He has the answer to *all* our problems: live according to His way. But, if we reject His offer, He cannot, without denying our freedom (and thus the merit of our love), force us to accept Him. Thus, He must leave us in our self-chosen misery of having rejected God Who is infinitely good. In a sense, He says, "If you change your mind, call Me."

This is how a person can choose Hell. In order to be free to love, we must be free to refuse to love. If God were to force us to love Him, we'd all be robots.

[24] Adapted from St. Francis de Sales, *Introduction to the Devout Life*, London: Rivingtons, 1876, part 1, chapter 15, pp. 41, 42, found at https://ccel.org/ccel/desales/devout_life/devout_life.iii.xv.html.

✠ ✠ ✠

Hell is real. As St. Augustine said, we can't get around the fact that there is a Hell and Jesus said people go there. Our primary focus should be on Heaven, but, when we become lazy about the spiritual life, we should heed the words of St. Bernard, St. Ignatius, and St. Francis de Sales: think about going to Hell. That should wake us up!

3

THE SUFFERING OF PURGATORY

WHAT IF YOU begin to grow in holiness, and you come to the point where you are in the state of grace, and you love God with *most* of your heart, soul, and mind but not all? And you love your neighbor *nearly* as much as you love yourself. And you die. Where would you go? Not to Heaven, since Jesus said you must love God with *all* your heart, soul, and mind, and your neighbor as yourself, to have everlasting life. You wouldn't go to Hell, either, since you died in the state of grace. You would go to Purgatory.

The dogma of Purgatory is an all but forgotten teaching of the Church, yet it is extremely valuable in supporting the call to perfection. The fundamental purpose of Purgatory is not the forgiveness of sins, but *atoning* for sins, reparation. The damage done by sin, especially to our own souls, is "repaired" in Purgatory.

When a boy accidentally throws a baseball through a neighbor's window, it is one thing to be forgiven by the owner, another thing to repair the window. When a man does something terrible to his wife, it is one thing to receive her forgiveness, quite another to make it up to her. True, Jesus has paid most of the price for sin, but we have a relatively small price to pay as well. St. Paul says, "Now I rejoice in my sufferings for your sake, and in my flesh I complete what is lacking in Christ's afflictions for the sake of his body, that is, the church" (Col. 1:24). So, there is a place or state we enter in order to repair the damage our sins have caused.

The biblical support for Purgatory is found, among other passages, in St. Paul:

> Each man's work will become manifest; for the Day will disclose it, because it will be revealed with fire, and the fire will test what sort of work each one has done. If the work which any man has built on the foundation survives, he will receive a reward. If anyone's work is burned up, he will suffer loss, though he himself will be saved, but only as through fire. (1 Cor. 3:13–15)[25]

So, Purgatory is a painful proposition, one that is not well known. It was defined as a dogma of the Church at the Council of Trent in 1563.[26] More recently, the *Catechism of the Catholic Church* teaches:

> The Church gives the name *Purgatory* to this final purification of the elect, which is entirely different from the punishment of the damned. The Church formulated her doctrine of faith on Purgatory especially at the Councils of Florence and Trent.

---

[25] Adapted from the RSV Bible, Catholic Edition. Some other Biblical passages which support the teaching on Purgatory: "And in anger his lord delivered him to the jailers, till he should pay all his debt. So also my heavenly Father will do to every one of you, if you do not forgive your brother from your heart" (Matt. 18:34–35). The implication here is that one may make up for sins after death. Also, in Maccabees we read, "Therefore, [Judas Maccabeus] made atonement for the dead, that they might be delivered from their sin" (2 Macc. 12:45). Prayer for the dead is linked to the doctrine of Purgatory, since if the dead are in Heaven or Hell, there is no need or no reason to pray for them. See also Matt. 12:32.

[26] Council of Trent, Session 25, December 3, 1563, Decree Concerning Purgatory; see *The Canons and Decrees of The Council of Trent*, trans. by H. J. Shroeder, OP, Rockford, IL: TAN Books, 1978, p. 214.

The tradition of the Church, by reference to certain texts of Scripture, speaks of a cleansing fire: "As for certain lesser faults, we must believe that, before the Final Judgment, there is a purifying fire." (CCC 1031)

St. Catherine of Genoa wrote: "The divine essence is so pure and light-filled — much more than we can imagine — that the soul that has but the slightest imperfection would rather throw itself into a thousand hells than appear thus before the divine presence."[27] And the Anglican, C. S. Lewis, wrote:

> Our souls *demand* Purgatory, don't they? Would it not break the heart if God said to us, "It is true, my son, that your breath smells and your rags drip with mud and slime, but we are charitable here and no one will upbraid you with these things, nor draw away from you. Enter into the joy."? Should we not reply, "With submission, sir, and if there is no objection, I'd rather be *cleaned* first." "It may hurt, you know." — "Even so, sir."[28]

To deny the doctrine of Purgatory would be to make hollow Christ's teaching that we must be made perfect, as our heavenly Father, or that we should love God with *all* our heart, soul, and mind, and love our neighbor *as* ourselves. Is it reasonable to think that if we fall far short of this perfection, but die in the state of grace, Jesus will meet us at the gates of Heaven and say, "That teaching on perfection (Matt. 5:48), I didn't really mean it. Come on in"?

[27] St. Catherine of Genoa, *Purgation and Purgatory, The Spiritual Dialogue*, Classics of Western Spirituality, Mahwah, NJ: Paulist Press, 1979, p. 78.

[28] C. S. Lewis, *Letters to Malcolm: Chiefly on Prayer*, chapter 20, nn. 7–10, pp. 108, 109, found at https://www.angelfire.com/pa3/OldWorldBasic/purgatorycslewis.htm. Author's emphasis.

THE PAIN AND JOY OF PURGATORY

St. Augustine wrote: "This fire of Purgatory will be more severe than any pain that can be felt, seen or conceived in this world."[29] St. Thomas Aquinas taught something similar:

> In Purgatory there will be a twofold loss, namely the delay of the divine vision, and the pain of sense, namely the punishment by bodily fire. With regard to both, the least pain of Purgatory surpasses the greatest pain of this life.[30]

St. Francis de Sales balances this misery with a certain sweetness for the souls in Purgatory:

> Their bitterest anguish is soothed by a certain profound peace. It is a species of Hell as regards the suffering; it is a Paradise as regards the delight infused into their hearts by charity—a charity stronger than death and more powerful than Hell.[31]

Why is there such joy in Purgatory? Because, once we are there, we are sure of entering Heaven one day. It's guaranteed.

Nonetheless, despite the delight of those being cleansed, the Church herself calls them the "Church Suffering," and I know of not one holy soul in Purgatory who has appeared to a saint—and several have appeared—and told them, "It's delightful here. Come and join me!" All have rather asked for prayers or penances or Masses to expedite their release.

---

[29] St. Thomas Aquinas, *Summa Theologica*, Supplement, App1 q1 a1, trans. by The Fathers of the English Dominican Province, New York: Benziger Bros., 1948, p. 3018.

[30] Ibid.

[31] St. Francis de Sales, *Esprit de Francis de Sales*, chapter 9, p. 16, found in F. X. Schouppe, S.J., *Purgatory: Explained by the Lives and Legends of the Saints,* Rockford, IL: TAN Books, 1986, p. 26.

THE HORROR OF SIN

Why is Purgatory so terribly painful? Because sin is so terribly horrible. Sin is totally incompatible with God, and, as Jesus showed us on the Cross, it is a painful thing to make reparation for it. Alas, we have lost the sense of sin, and with it the harshness of Purgatory.

St. Ignatius of Loyola proposed as a "second mode of humility" that we come to say, "[I would not] for the sake of all creation, or for the purpose of saving my life, consider committing a single venial sin."[32] St. Catherine of Genoa wrote:

> When I beheld that vision in which I saw the magnitude of the stain of even one least sin against God, I know not why I did not die. I said: I no longer marvel that hell is so horrible, since it was made for sin; for even hell (as I have seen it) I do not believe to be really proportionate to the dreadfulness of sin; on the contrary, it seems to me that even in hell God is very merciful, since I have beheld the terrible stain caused by but one venial sin.[33]

St. Francis of Assisi said, "Even though I had committed but one little sin, I should have ample reason to repent of it all my life."[34] Cardinal Newman wrote:

---

[32] St. Ignatius of Loyola, *The Spiritual Exercises of Saint Ignatius*, trans. by Anthony Mottola, Garden City, NY: Image Books, 1964, 2nd week, 12th day, p. 82.

[33] St. Catherine of Genoa, *Life and Doctrine of Saint Catherine of Genoa*, chapter 22, found in *Life and Doctrine of Saint Catherine of Genoa*, New York: Christian Press Association, 1907, found at https://ccel.org/ccel/catherine_g/life/life.iv.xxii.html.

[34] See "Reflections: St. Francis of Assisi," from MyCatholicSource.com, found at http://www.mycatholicsource.com/mcs/qt/saint_francis_reflections_teachings.htm.

The Catholic Church holds it better for the sun and moon to drop from heaven, for the earth to fail, and for all the many millions on it to die of starvation in extremest agony, as far as temporal affliction goes, than that one soul, I will not say, should be lost, but should commit one single venial sin, should tell one willful untruth, or should steal one poor farthing without excuse.[35]

Pope John Paul II taught regarding Purgatory in August of 1999:

We are invited to "cleanse ourselves from every defilement of body and spirit" (2 Cor. 7:1; cf. 1 John 3:3), because the encounter with God requires absolute purity.

Every trace of attachment to evil must be eliminated, every imperfection of the soul corrected. Purification must be complete, and indeed this is precisely what is meant by the Church's teaching on *purgatory*.[36]

Every time we sin, mortally or venially, we add to the debt. Can we "pay the debt" here on earth? Indeed, we can! St. Teresa of Ávila said, "Let us praise God and strive to do penance in this life. How sweet will be the death of those who have done penance for all their sins, and [need] not to go to Purgatory!"[37]

Pope Paul VI taught the following:

---

[35] St. John Henry Newman, *Apologia Pro Vita Sua*, London: Longman, Green, Longmans, Roberts, and Green, 1864, p. 384. https://www.google.com/books/edition/_/rQ5GAAAAcAAJ?gbpv=1&bsq=one%20single%20venial%20sin

[36] Pope John Paul II, General Audience, August 4, 1999, n. 5, found at https://www.ewtn.com/catholicism/library/heaven-hell-and-purgatory-8222.

[37] St. Teresa of Ávila, *The Way of Perfection*, chapter 40, p. 266.

The truth has been divinely revealed that sins bring punishments inflicted by God's sanctity and justice. These must be expiated either on this earth through the sorrows, miseries and calamities of this life, and above all, through death, or else in the life beyond, through fire and torments or "purifying" punishments.[38]

And, how much better it is to pay the debt in this life! St. Catherine of Genoa wrote, "He who purifies himself from his faults in the present life satisfies with a penny a debt of a thousand [silver pieces]"[39]

THE "DURATION" OF PURGATORY

St. Robert Bellarmine, Doctor of the Church, wrote, "There is no doubt that the pains of Purgatory are not limited to ten or twenty years, and that they last in some cases entire centuries."[40] And, it seems that to the souls in Purgatory the time seems — or is — much longer than the equivalent time on earth. St. Catherine of Genoa wrote, "If we regarded our own proper good, it would seem better to us to suffer here for a little than to remain in torments forever; better to suffer for a thousand years every woe possible to this body in this world, than to remain one hour in purgatory."[41]

---

[38] Pope Paul VI, *Apostolic Constitution on the Revision of Indulgences*, January 1, 1967, n. 2, found in USCCB, *Manual of Indulgences*, Washington, DC: 2006, p. 122.

[39] F. X. Schouppe, S.J., *Purgatory: Explained by the Lives and Legends of the Saints*, p. 287.

[40] St. Robert Bellarmine, *De Genitu*, lib. ii. c. 9, found in F. X. Schouppe, S.J., *Purgatory: Explained by the Lives and Legends of the Saints*, p. 68.

[41] St. Catherine of Genoa, *Spiritual Dialogue*, chapter 16, found in *Life and Doctrine of Saint Catherine of Genoa*, found at https://ccel.org/ccel/catherine_g/life/life.v.i.xvi.html

Bl. James Alberione, founder of the Society of St. Paul and the Daughters of St. Paul, wrote:

> Regarding the duration of the pains of the suffering souls, we can recall some things which make us think deeply and fear greatly.... Absolute duration is one thing, and relative duration is another. The first is the time which the soul really spends in Purgatory; the second is the impression that the soul has of this time. That is, the soul which suffers but briefly believes that it has been suffering for a long time. Many revelations say that only an hour in Purgatory seems longer than a century.[42]

We speak of time in Purgatory only analogously. Fr. Reginald Garrigou-Lagrange, a noted twentieth-century theologian, commented:

> Theological opinion, in general, favors long duration of purgatorial purification. Private revelations mention three or four centuries, or even more, especially for those who have had high office and great responsibility.... Purgatory is not measured by solar time, but by eviternity and discontinuous time. Discontinuous time ... is composed of successive spiritual instants, and each of these instants may correspond to ten, twenty, thirty, sixty hours of our solar time.[43]

(Eviternity, or *aeviternity*, according to St. Thomas Aquinas, "differs from time, and from eternity, as the mean between them both" [*Summa Theologiae*, I q10 a5]).

---

[42] Bl. James Alberione, *Lest We Forget*, Boston, MA: Daughters of St. Paul, 1967, p. 77.

[43] Reginald Garrigou-Lagrange, *Life Everlasting & the Immensity of the Soul: A Theological Treatise on the Four Last Things: Death, Judgment, Heaven, Hell*, Rockford, IL: TAN Books, 1991, p 176, 177.

So this is the sad fate of those who fail to take seriously the need to strive for perfection, or who take it seriously and don't quite make it but die in the state of grace: a miserably painful existence for however many (analogous) months, or years or centuries it takes. And, the time in Purgatory is much longer than its equivalent here on earth.

CONFESSION

You might ask, "What happens to a person who goes to Confession, does his penance, and is killed on his way home? Where would he most likely go?" Not to Heaven. Most likely to Purgatory.

"But he completed his penance," you say. Yes, but some historical perspective is needed here. In the fourth and fifth centuries, the penance for one of the three major sins — murder, adultery or fornication, or denying the Faith — was truly severe. You might have to spend ten or fifteen years in penance for one instance of these, and, if you were married, you could never again have relations with your spouse. If you were not married, you could never *get* married.

Needless to say, people guilty of these things were not coming in great numbers to go to Confession. They would put off going to Confession as long as possible, usually until their deathbed.

It appears that the Church noted this and began to ease up on the penances. It seems it was deemed best to get people forgiven as soon as possible, to preserve them from losing their souls, even if the penances had to be reduced considerably. The penances became more and more symbolic, not representing all that might be needed to make up for the sins confessed.

Thus, for most people, going to Confession and doing the penance will not prepare them to enter the Kingdom. Some, who are particularly holy, could go directly to Heaven, but for most it would ordinarily take a great deal more.

THE SAINTS' EXPERIENCES

At one point, Don Bernardino de Mendoza, the brother of the bishop of Ávila, had given St. Teresa of Ávila a house near Valladolid to found a new convent there. While she was at Alcalá Teresa received news of his death. The Lord told her this man had been in danger of losing his soul, but Mary had interceded for him in gratitude for his donating the house for her order, and he was in Purgatory. He would remain there until the first Mass occurred in that new house.[44]

Although she made every effort to expedite the founding of the new convent, she had to wait several months. When she finally had the first Mass said in the convent, she saw Bernardino standing next to the priest as she received Communion. He appeared in glory and thanked her for his release from Purgatory.[45]

In November 1856, John Bosco's beloved mother and longtime helper died. Four years later, she appeared to him. He asked her, "Are you happy?" Her reply was, "Very happy." He then asked, "Did you go straight to Heaven when you died?" "No," was her abrupt response. Even this saintly woman — great holiness we must attain, by God's grace, in order to enter heaven.[46]

St. Margaret Mary wrote of a Benedictine monk who appeared to her in a "pitiable condition," in fire of which she herself felt the

---

[44] St. Teresa of Ávila, *Foundations*, found in *The Collected Works of St. Teresa of Ávila*, vol. III, trans. by Keiran Kavanaugh, O.C.D. and Otilio Rodriguez, O.C.D., Washington, D.C.: ICS Publications, 1976, p. 145; and Marcelle Auclair, *Teresa of Ávila*, New York: Pantheon Books, 1953, pp. 188, 189.

[45] St. Teresa of Ávila, *Foundations*, found in *The Collected Works of St. Teresa of Ávila*, vol. III, p. 146.

[46] Peter Lappin, *Give Me Souls! Life of Don Bosco*, New Rochelle, NY: Don Bosco Publications, 1986, p. 188.

heat. He told her that because he had directed her to receive holy Communion, he was given the grace to approach her and ask her to offer her sufferings and actions for him for three months to ease his sufferings. He told her he was in Purgatory because: he was too concerned about others' opinions of him, he was too attached to other people and he was not as charitable to his fellow monks as he should have been. She received permission from her superior to do as the monk asked. And she endured terrible suffering, feeling the heat from his presence, which continued for the whole three months. After this he appeared to her in glory, about to enter Heaven, and promised to help her from there.[47]

St. Teresa of Ávila related two experiences relative to the holy souls:

> Eighteen or twenty years ago another nun died in the house I was in. She had always been sick and been a very good servant of God, devoted to her choir duties and most virtuous. I thought certainly she would not enter purgatory, because the illnesses she had suffered were many, and that she would have a surplus of merits. Four hours after her death, while reciting the hours of the Office before her burial, I understood she departed from purgatory and went to heaven.[48]

> Another friar of our order, a truly very good friar, was seriously ill; while I was at Mass I became recollected and saw that he was dead and that he ascended into heaven without entering purgatory. He died at the hour I saw him,

---

[47] St. Margaret Mary Alacoque, *The Autobiography of Saint Margaret Mary*, p. 110.

[48] St. Teresa of Ávila, *The Book of Her Life*, found in *The Collected Works of St. Teresa of Ávila*, p. 266.

according to what I learned later. I was amazed he hadn't entered purgatory. I understood that since he had been a friar who had observed his vows well, the Bulls of the order about not entering purgatory were beneficial to him.[49]

Teresa said, based on her visions, she was not aware of any soul who had gone directly to Heaven besides the friar she mentioned above, St. Peter of Alcántara, and one Dominican priest.[50]

In summary, then, Purgatory is a difficult prospect. If we fail to take seriously Jesus' call to perfection, we can anticipate much suffering. God does not want us to go to Purgatory; He urges us to give totally of ourselves, to become holy, to become totally loving—and *happy* in His Kingdom! May we heed His call!

---

[49] Ibid., pp. 266, 267.
[50] Ibid., p. 267.

4

THE PURSUIT OF HAPPINESS

Every intelligent human being pursues happiness. No one in his right mind is intentionally seeking to be miserable. The key to finding this happiness is, of course, to seek it in the right places.

Anyone who knows the Christian faith realizes that *eternal* happiness lies only with God and in fulfilling His two great commandments of love. However, some have wondered if perhaps we must live boring, miserable lives on this earth in order to fulfill those commandments and then will be rewarded with happiness when we die. In fact, nothing could be further from the truth.

If we look closely at the lives of the saints, we see very happy people, people who were truly fulfilled. St. Francis of Assisi comes to mind immediately as someone who had virtually nothing in this world, but was very joyful. St. John Bosco, St. Teresa of Ávila, St. Thérèse of Lisieux, St. John of the Cross, St. Dominic Savio, to name a few, they were all happy. They found the "pearl of great price" and it filled them with joy.

SCRIPTURE AND HAPPINESS

Sacred Scripture proclaims over and over the happiness that results from loving God

> "Happy are we, O Israel, for we know what is pleasing to God." (Bar. 4:4)

Blessed is the man
who walks not in the counsel of the wicked,
nor stands in the way of sinners,
nor sits in the seat of scoffers;
but his delight is in the law of the LORD,
and on his law he meditates day and night.
He is like a tree
planted by streams of water,
that yields its fruit in its season,
and its leaf does not wither.
In all that he does, he prospers. (Ps. 1:1–3)

Happy the people whose God is the LORD!
　　(Ps. 144:15)

Happy is he whose help is the God of Jacob,
whose hope is in the LORD his God. (Ps. 146:5)

EARTHLY FULFILLMENT

Those who reject God tend to seek happiness in worldly things, such as pleasure, honor, comfort, or wealth. However, if we look closely at the lives of those who have these things, we often find an emptiness—if not downright unhappiness and misery. There is a richness, a profundity that these things lack, a richness which the human heart seems to be made for. This is why so many people who seem to have so many of this world's goods fall into depression or drug or alcohol abuse.

It seems that there are two things which fulfill us as persons. The first is knowing that we have made the lives of other people better. Not just more pleasant, but truly better. We call this love. The second is drawing close to others. This is called *intimacy*. Intimacy often follows love, and it is its proper crown. But even if intimacy sometimes doesn't follow, it is still rewarding to know you have made another person's life better.

Although these two bring us pleasure, it is not the pleasure which fulfills us, but the things themselves, since they nourish the human heart. As Aristotle taught, pleasure is good only if it accompanies a morally good act. Pleasure is a fleeting thing, even if it comes from doing what is good.

It is no accident that Christianity provides both love and intimacy par excellence. Loving God and neighbor is absolutely necessary for entry into the Kingdom. When a Christian does these things, he is fulfilling his human nature. He is doing what brings happiness.

Pope John Paul II put it well:

> Man cannot live without love. He remains a being that is incomprehensible for himself, his life is senseless, if love is not revealed to him, if he does not encounter love, if he does not experience it and make it his own, if he does not participate intimately in it.[51]

Vatican II said something similar:

> The Lord Jesus, when He prayed to the Father, "that all may be one … as we are one" (John 17:21–22) opened up vistas closed to human reason, for He implied a certain likeness between the union of the divine Persons, and the unity of God's sons in truth and charity. This likeness reveals that man, who is the only creature on earth which God willed for itself, cannot fully find himself except through a sincere gift of himself.[52]

---

[51] Pope St. John Paul II, *Redemptor Hominis* (The Redeemer of Man), March 4, 1979, n. 25, found at https://www.ewtn.com/catholicism/library/redeemer-of-man-3393.

[52] Vatican II, *Gaudium et Spes* (Consistution on the Church in the Modern World), December 7, 1965, n. 24, found at https://www.ewtn.com/catholicism/library/pastoral-constitution-on-the-church-in-the-modern-world-1529.

By fulfilling the two commandments of love, the human person finds intimacy. Anyone who prays a good deal, receives the sacraments, attends Mass regularly, and strives to grow in virtue will find himself very close to God. He will have a personal relationship with the God Who loves him tenderly and passionately. He will also receive the power to love others as God loves them, unconditionally, and this will almost always bring about intimacy with these persons, especially those who are virtuous. Intimacy with the virtuous is a true joy.

Thus, no one should think that we will have happiness only in Heaven. It begins here. In fact, not only does Heaven begin on earth for those who live the Gospel, but Hell begins here as well for those who don't.

Let us strive for heavenly happiness, and know that the journey is hard, but sweet.

PART II

The Life of Grace

5

THE TWO GREAT COMMANDMENTS OF LOVE

HOW DO WE get to the Kingdom? Some suggest that being a "good guy," not being mean or nasty to others is enough. Others propose that helping others will do it. Still others claim that avoiding sin is what is needed. Happily, there need not be any mystery about what it takes. Jesus answered that very question:

> A lawyer stood up to put him to the test, saying, "Teacher, what shall I do to inherit eternal life?" He said to him, "What is written in the law? How do you read?" And he answered, "You shall love the Lord your God with all your heart, and with all your soul, and with all your strength, and with all your mind; and your neighbor as yourself." And he said to him, "You have answered right; do this, and you will live." (Luke 10:25–28)

But how do we love God? And how do we love our neighbor? What exactly is meant by this word *love*?

The Greek word used in the Gospel here is *agape*. Pope Benedict XVI wrote:

> By contrast with an indeterminate, "searching" love, this word [*agape*] expresses the experience of a love which involves a real discovery of the other, moving beyond the

selfish character that prevailed earlier. Love now becomes concern and care for the other. No longer is it self-seeking, a sinking in the intoxication of happiness; instead it seeks the good of the beloved: it becomes renunciation and it is ready, and even willing, for sacrifice.[53]

We might define this love as a *giving of self for the good of the beloved without conditions*; or, *an unconditional active benevolence for the beloved*. Certainly, this is how God loves us.

Notice, it's not just an indiscriminate giving but a giving only if it is good for the one who receives it. I met a woman once who gave her son everything. Even in his mid-twenties she provided him with a place to stay without cost. She lent him money which he never paid back. She gave him everything he asked for, and he became less and less able to do things for himself. To make matters worse, the more she gave him, the more he resented her (a common phenomenon). He treated her terribly.

It was only when she told him to move out that he finally found a job, and began to stand on his own two feet. Her excessive giving to her son, who was quite capable of supporting himself, had held him back and made him dependent on her.

Not all giving is love. In fact, some giving is done merely for self-gratification. In order to be love, the giving must always be for the good of the recipient. This is why God often refuses us what we ask for. St. James put it well: "You ask and do not receive, because you ask wrongly, to spend it on your passions" (James 4:3).

And, as we said earlier, this love is unconditional. The act of concern for the good of the other is not tied to their behavior or

---

[53] Pope Benedict XVI, *Deus Caritas Est* (On Christian Love), December 25, 2005, n. 6, found at https://www.ewtn.com/catholicism/library/deus-caritas-est-3354.

their looks or even their good health. The Christian spouse says on the wedding day, "I will love you for better or for worse." This means unconditionally. When things really do get worse, this may not be much fun, but it is the only way human love can image divine love. And it is the only way to find happiness.

Loving God in this agapaic way can be spoken of slightly differently than loving creatures. To love God as He commands is to give of ourselves to *please Him* without conditions. Only what is truly good will please God. Loving God is the sure way to live in the state of grace.

There is something in this definition that should teach us the way to approach God. It should be *unconditional.* Sometimes we turn from God because He does not answer our prayers as we would like, or He allows terrible things to happen in our lives. But if we are to love in the way He has taught us—by His own example—we should continue to pray without condition, especially the prayers of thanksgiving and adoration.

There are other types of love that are more exciting, more stimulating. Emotional love, *eros*, the desire for the good, the beautiful, and the true in the other, is thrilling, but not divine. Friendship, *philia*, is very worthwhile, and is at the heart of a good marriage, but it needs divine love to undergird it. Affection, *storge*, is a beautiful art which enriches lives, but, without divine love, it can become selfish.

It is *agape* that we spoke of in the previous chapter, the love that fulfills us and the love that often leads to intimacy. Jesus promised that it would involve a cross, that it would be hard, but He promised to lighten the load. There is no salvation without this love.

LOVING GOD

How do we love God? We begin the same way we begin to love others here on earth: by communication. No one can say they love God if they do not communicate with Him. This communication with God is called prayer.

Prayer is not the only way to love God. We love Him by seeking His forgiveness in the Sacrament of Penance and Reconciliation, by seeking His intimacy and encouragement in the Sacrament of the Eucharist; and we love Him by receiving His grace in each of the sacraments.

But, we love Him most powerfully by participating in the Holy Sacrifice of the Mass, the commemoration and re-offering of the sacrifice of Jesus on the Cross. It is there that we participate in the "source and summit of the church's life and mission"[54] and, "as from a font, grace is poured forth upon us."[55]

LOVING NEIGHBOR

And how do we love our neighbor? Primarily, through the spiritual and corporal works of mercy and by being kind, polite, gracious, and thoughtful. To love our neighbor *as ourselves* means to be concerned for the good of our neighbor as much as we are concerned for our own good.

WITH *ALL* OUR HEART

It is one thing to love God, but to love Him with all our heart, soul, strength, and mind — that's big. God doesn't expect us to keep holy His day only when we don't have shopping to do, or a soccer game to attend, or a party to go to. He expects us to arrange our day — or our weekend if necessary — around the commitment to worship

[54] Pope Benedict XVI, *Sacramentum caritatis* (On the Eucharist as the Source and Summit of the Church's Life and Mission), February 22, 2007, nn. 3, 17, 70, 77, 84, 93, found at https://www.ewtn.com/catholicism/library/sacramentum-caritatis-6930.

[55] Vatican II, *Sacrosanctum Concilium* (Constitution on the Sacred Liturgy), December 4, 1963, n. 10, found at https://www.ewtn.com/catholicism/library/sacrosanctum-concilium-constitution-on-the-sacred-liturgy-1525.

Him on Sunday. If we can't get to Mass on Sunday morning, we should get there Saturday evening or Sunday evening.

When we travel, we should figure out in advance how we will get to Mass on Sunday. I know a layman who traveled through England (hardly a Catholic country) for a week and was able to attend Mass not only on Sunday, but every day! With the Internet, it's easy to find Masses nearby at many different hours.[56] Certainly when we're sick, or find ourselves unavoidably far from a church, we are excused. However, some seem to have many excuses for missing Sunday Mass, and others rarely need an excuse. It's often about priorities.

If we truly love God this intensely, we will make our prayer life a priority throughout the week, not just on Sundays. Even if we are just starting to pray, and are only committed to five or ten minutes a day, we will plan our day around those few minutes. We will make considerable sacrifices to be sure and complete our prayers. If we have to excuse ourselves from visiting friends for a short time, or take the trouble to arrange a ride to church, so be it. When we're in love, we find a way.

Granted, loving God may not at first involve the same emotional pull as being in love with someone on earth, but it should involve the same zeal. In one case the zeal is felt; in the other, the zeal is willed. And, happily, if we will the zeal for communicating with and worshiping God, in time we *will* feel it. *That* is the pearl of great price.

It is this sort of commitment that inspires a layman to be able to say, "By the grace of God, I've missed Sunday (or *daily*) Mass only five times in the last ten years, all for sickness." Or a priest to be able to say, "By God's grace I have said Mass every day for thirty

---

[56] See www.masstimes.org for the times of Masses at the ten closest churches to the location you enter.

years." Archbishop Fulton Sheen used to say, "I have been blessed to make a eucharistic holy hour every day for over fifty years."

Loving God with all our heart, soul, strength, and mind is about priorities and making a commitment to spend a certain amount of time with Him daily. If we don't have a commitment we are in essence saying, "Lord, I will pray when I have time." That's not making God first. There is no excuse for failing to make God our first priority. And, no one has ever regretted doing so in the end.

6

THE FOUNDATION: PRAYER

AT THE END of World War II, the Russian army took over Austria. For three years they occupied that country, but then a priest by the name of Fr. Petrus began a Rosary crusade in the country. He urged everyone to pray the Rosary for their deliverance from Russian rule. His goal was to get 10 percent of the country to pledge to it, and the people of Austria responded just as he had hoped: seven hundred thousand Austrians began to pray the Rosary every day. After seven years of rosaries, on May 13, 1955,[57] inexplicably by human terms, the Russian army left Austria.[58] Prayer is a most powerful tool against evil!

Is prayer primarily about asking for what we want? No, but it certainly should include that. The Lord does expect us to ask for things we need in prayer. In fact, He said:

> Ask, and it will be given you; seek, and you will find; knock, and it will be opened to you. For every one who asks receives, and he who seeks finds, and to him who knocks it will be opened. . . . If you then, who are evil, know how to give good

---

[57] May 13 was the date of the first apparition of Mary at Fatima. It was at one of the subsequent apparitions there that Mary predicted the Russian takeover of many countries.

[58] Albert Shamon, *The Power of The Rosary*, Oak Lawn, IL: CMJ Marian Publishers, 1990, pp. 30, 31.

gifts to your children, how much more will the heavenly Father give the Holy Spirit to those who ask him! (Luke 11:9–10, 13)

But this is not the only reason to pray. Prayer is our way of coming to know God and to love Him. We come to God to thank Him, to seek His forgiveness, to adore Him, and yes, to ask Him for what we need. Indeed, prayer is the foundation of our entire life with the Lord; everything we do in this life rests on this foundation of communication with God.

What exactly is prayer? Prayer is simply lifting up the mind and heart to God. Or, to put it differently, it is communicating with God. St. Thérèse, the Little Flower, put it as follows: "For me, prayer is an upward leap of the heart, an untroubled glance towards heaven, a cry of gratitude and love which I utter from the depths of sorrow as well as the heights of joy. It has a supernatural grandeur which expands the soul and unites it with God."[59]

MOTIVES FOR PRAYER

There are four motives for prayer: adoration, contrition, thanksgiving, and petition or supplication (thus the acronym, ACTS). Certainly, adoration is the highest motive for prayer, in general, but all four motives should be practiced. The Psalms, 150 songs addressed to God, are a model for prayer. And they include all of the four motives. We often find the psalmist petitioning or asking God for help. For example:

Incline thy ear to me,
     rescue me speedily!
Be thou a rock of refuge for me,
     a strong fortress to save me!

[59] St. Thérèse of Lisieux, *The Autobiography of St. Thérèse of Lisieux: The Story of a Soul*, trans. by John Beevers, Garden City, NY: Image Books, 1957, p. 136.

Yea, thou art my rock and my fortress;

for thy name's sake lead me and guide me.

(Ps. 31:2–3)

PETITION

Why does God encourage us to ask for things in prayer? For several reasons. First, God wants us to be deeply aware that all good things come from Him. What better way than to invite us to seek His help in any need!

Second, God no doubt wants us to be humble enough to be aware of our neediness and to constantly realize that, no matter what spiritual heights we might reach, we are utterly dependent on Him for everything. Furthermore, God wants to manifest His presence and to reward our faith by answering our prayers. This He does, sometimes in dramatic ways. This is a way of encouraging our faith. Many, many people have had their faith boosted by an answer to prayer.

I once met a young woman who was one of thirteen children and almost all of them attended Mass and prayed the Rosary every day. I asked her to what she attributed this apparent faith among herself and her brothers and sisters. She said that when they were young they would all pray the Rosary together as a family for special intentions, and their prayers were almost always answered. Thus, turning to God in times of need became a habit for them. God wants us to get in the habit of communicating with Him. What better way than to appeal to one of our most basic instincts, our needs and desires!

Of course, we should understand *how* we are to ask for things and what we can expect. For example, Christ said: "If two of you agree on earth about anything they ask, it will be done for them by my Father in heaven" (Matt. 18:19). Would this include a prayer asking for the death of a business competitor? No, God Who is good only grants good requests. That is why, at the end of any prayer in which we request something, we should add the words: "If it be for my good," or, "If it be your will."

Thomas Merton began praying in earnest that he would have a novel he wrote accepted for publication. That novel was never accepted. But, this began his habit of prayer, which was far more valuable than getting a book published.

When I was a young man, working as an engineer, I used to pray for relief from difficult love relationships. The Lord gave me relief, and in gratitude I continued praying hard long after such relationships ended. As a result, I found a relationship with God which has far exceeded the relationships I had been seeking.

Perhaps this little poem by an unknown confederate soldier could help us understand how we pray and how God answers us:

I asked God for strength, that I might achieve;
I was made weak, that I might humbly learn to obey.
I asked for health, that I might do greater things;
I was given infirmity, that I might do better things.
I asked for riches, that I might be happy;
I was given poverty, that I might be wise.
I asked for power, that I might have the praise of men;
I was given weakness, that I might feel the need of God.
I asked for all things, that I might enjoy life;
I was given life, that I might enjoy all things.
I received nothing that I asked for —
but everything that I had hoped for;
Almost despite myself, my unspoken prayers were answered.
I am, among all men, most richly blessed.[60]

---

[60] See Unknown, "A Creed for Those Who Have Suffered," from Bartleby.com, found at https://www.bartleby.com/73/1477.html.

It seems that if God does not give us what we ask for He gives us something better. St. Thérèse wrote, "I no longer know how to ask passionately for anything, except that the Will of God shall be perfectly accomplished in my soul."[61] This is what it means to really pray, as a saint: to pray that the will of God shall be perfectly accomplished in our souls—and, of course, that we accept His will.

THANKSGIVING

The motive of thanksgiving in prayer is extremely important. We are reminded to give thanks to God over forty times in the Psalms. Psalm 136 is a good example. It begins with the verse, "Give thanks to the LORD, for he is good, for his steadfast love endures forever," and then goes on for the next twenty-five verses to enumerate the reasons why we should give Him thanks. When our Lord healed the ten lepers, He lamented the fact that only one returned to give thanks for His healing (Luke 17:11–19). The word *thanks* appears fifty-eight times in the Old Testament thirty-three times in the New; *thanksgiving* appears eighty-three and forty-eight times, respectively.

We should be immensely thankful to God at every moment of every day. If we think clearly about our lives, most of us can find many, many things to thank God for. For family, for friends, for intelligence, for health, for food and drink, for the beauty of the world, for our very existence. All of us have experienced at least some of these things.

I was once working with a young woman who was depressed. It was clear to me that she didn't have enough spiritual energy to pray the Rosary daily, but she knew she needed to pray. I urged her to thank God for at least seven things every day, and to be quite specific about just what these things were. She began to do so, and I believe

---

[61] St. Thérèse of Lisieux, *The Autobiography of St. Thérèse of Lisieux: The Story of a Soul*, p. 109.

she drew closer to God each day. She became more and more positive. After some months of that she overcame some of her depression and was able to pray the Rosary daily. Since that time, I have made every effort to take some of my own medicine, and thank God all day long.

Some people have such wonderful gifts as a good and faithful spouse, good children, good parents, good health, a good job, a holy pastor, and any number of other good things—none of which they could claim to deserve—and they begin to take them for granted. Then, when one of these is taken away, they become angry at God for letting them down. What ingratitude!

Do we really believe God owes us all these things? This is not to downplay the deep emotional hurt that often occurs when we lose someone or something very dear to us, but, do we really have a right to be angry at God for losing one of so many gifts? Be sad, and ask for His consolation, but do not be angry. We should be thankful for the gifts we still have, especially our greatest gift, His friendship.

What follows is a prayer of thanks which we should say often:

PRAYER OF THANKS

Heavenly Father, I thank You for my very existence, which You gave me out of the abundance of Your love, and which You sustain at every moment. I thank You for my health, which I so often take for granted, and for my family, which I also take for granted. I thank You for my intellect, by which You enable me to think, and for my will, by which You enable me to love. Thank You for my body, and the food and drink by which You sustain it, and the shelter by which You protect it. Thank You for my soul, and the grace of Your Holy Spirit, by which You nourish it. My every talent comes from You, my every possession, my every moment of time, for which I will be eternally grateful.

Thank You for Blessed Mary, who intercedes for me before You. And, thank You most of all for Jesus, Who has given us new life, new hope, new love by His death and Resurrection, and for the Church which brings Him to us each day.

What an awesome, generous, loving God You are! You ask me to worship You at least weekly and to pray to You without ceasing. It is my privilege and my joy to do so in thanksgiving for all You have given me. Amen.

If God gave us nothing more than our existence, and the *chance*, the *opportunity* to learn to love Him and our neighbor, that we might experience the beauty and goodness of Love Himself in an eternal, intimate embrace, we would have reason to thank Him. If He never answered another prayer, we would still have reason to be grateful to Him for all eternity.

In the United States, we have one day a year dedicated to thanksgiving. It's good that we have such a day, but, every day should be a day to thank God for the many blessings He has given us. The Church celebrates "thanksgiving" every day: that is the meaning of the word *Eucharist*. It would seem that thanking God always is an integral part of holiness. As the angel told Tobit and his father,

> Praise God and give thanks to him; exalt him and give thanks to him in the presence of all the living for what he has done for you. It is good to praise God and to exalt his name, worthily declaring the works of God. Do not be slow to give him thanks." (Tob. 12:6)

CONTRITION

Contrition, or sorrow for sins, is another motivation for prayer. Psalm 51 is a classic example of the prayer of contrition: "Have mercy on me, O God, according to thy steadfast love; according to thy abundant mercy blot out my transgressions. Wash me thoroughly from my iniquity, and cleanse me from my sin!" (Ps. 51:1–2). This Psalm, also known as the *Miserere* or Prayer of Repentance, goes on in this vein for nineteen verses.

Near the end of his life St. John Vianney used to say that he wanted to retire from his parish and go to some monastery to weep for his sins. The holier we become, the more deeply we are aware of our sins.

Contrition is so important in our Church that we have a sacrament in which to express it. No doubt God knew our psychological need to alleviate our reasonable guilt, to express our sorrow, and to seek forgiveness.

It seems that today many have lost a sense of sin, an awareness that we have done something wrong and need to change our ways. At the same time, we sense that something is not right. Could it be that we have … sinned?

We need not obsess over our sins, but we should have a healthy awareness of sin, our sin. One way to accomplish that is to make a list of our three (or fewer) most prevalent sins and look at that list each night and pray an Act of Contrition before going to bed.

ADORATION

Finally, adoration, the highest motive for prayer, is simply an outpouring of praise and love for God. Again, we find over and over the praises of God sung in the Psalms: "Ascribe to the LORD, O heavenly beings, ascribe to the LORD glory and strength. Ascribe to the LORD the glory of his name; worship the LORD in holy array." (Ps. 29:1–2). (Incidentally, that last phrase "worship the LORD in holy array" is something we should remember as we dress for Sunday Mass.)

When we think of it, we have very little to offer God in return for His many wonderful gifts. He has *everything*, and yet we know that He delights in our words of praise and adoration. When we pray the prayer of adoration, He allows us to get close to Him, to be His intimate lover.

Think of how praise affects you. When others praise you, don't you feel good? Don't you usually thank them for those words of praise? Don't you feel a bit closer to them?

A child who receives constant criticism from his parents develops low esteem and will have little self-confidence. But, if he receives frequent praise, he is likely to flourish and to behave better and better. The person who often praises his or her spouse will often reap abundant rewards very quickly.

Thus, it should be no surprise that this praise and adoration of God should please Him and move Him to bless us. And, there is no limit to the things we can praise God for: His kindness, His amazing mercy, His beauty, His generosity, His wisdom, His glorious power, His infinite love … We find some of the best prayers of adoration and praise in the Psalms. Perhaps this is why the Church prescribes that priests and religious pray the Psalms at least five times a day in the Divine Office (also known as the Liturgy of the Hours).

May we never tire of running to God when we are in need, thanking Him for all He has given to us, throwing ourselves on His mercy when we have done wrong, and adoring Him in our every waking moment. He has given us every good thing we have, and He has invited us to be His spouse forever in His Kingdom.

METHODS OF PRAYER

Now, what are some of the methods of prayer? Certainly, one which is familiar to all is vocal prayer, or formal prayer. In vocal prayer we follow a set formula such as in the Our Father or the Psalms, and we allow our hearts and minds to be lifted up to God through these words. Another less formal method is simply to speak to God in our own words, telling Him of our troubles, our joys, our needs, and our desires. This is typically called conversation. A third method of prayer is meditation, that is, thinking about the Word of God or events in the life of Christ. Sometimes called mental prayer, this is considered a richer type of prayer than vocal prayer or conversation with God. We will dedicate the next chapter to meditative prayer and to contemplative prayer (something God works in us).

VOCAL PRAYER

"Vocal prayer, founded on the union of body and soul in human nature, associates the body with the interior prayer of the heart, following Christ's example of praying to his Father and teaching the Our Father to his disciples" (CCC 2722). To put it more simply, vocal prayer is praying a set formula.

Presumably, most of us say the Our Father every day, but do we really know what it means, and do we think about what it means?

This is a necessary element of a prayer from the heart—knowing what you are saying, and thinking about it when you pray. Any other way is a kind of thoughtless recitation of words that is not very pleasing to God.

THE OUR FATHER

What exactly does the Our Father mean? The first word, *Our*, reminds us that the Lord would have us pray with others. St. John Chrysostom taught, "[The Lord] teaches us to make prayer in common for all our brethren. For he did not say 'my Father' who art in heaven, but 'our' Father, offering petitions for the common body."[62] In fact, Jesus is so pleased to see us pray together that He joins us: "Where two or three are gathered in my name, there am I in the midst of them." (Matt. 18:20). If Jesus prays with us, we shall certainly be heard! St. Francis de Sales said, "God has ordained that communion in prayer must always be preferred to every form of private prayer."[63]

The word *Father* reminds us of the intimacy God wishes to have with us. He is not merely a king or emperor or teacher, but our own Father. And, He is the perfect Father. If on earth we had a father who was not so great, we can discover perfect fatherhood by getting to know God, especially in the Psalms. We are His sons and daughters. He loves us passionately, unconditionally. He cares for us and has counted every hair on our heads (Luke 12:7).

"Who art in Heaven, hallowed be Thy name": In other words, may Your name be held holy by all. And, we are asking not only

---

[62] St. John Chrysostom, *Hom. in Mt.* 19, 4: PG 57, 278, as found in CCC 2768.

[63] St. Francis de Sales, *Introduction to the Devout Life*, trans. by John K. Ryan, New York: Harper & Brothers, 1950, part 2, chapter 15, p. 102.

that God's name be held holy, but that the entire Person of God be held holy. In Scripture, when the term "your name" is used, it refers to the person as a whole. We speak of "calling on your name," "glorifying your name," and "loving your name" in the Psalms. When the apostles were beaten and told not to speak about Jesus by the Sanhedrin, they rejoiced that "they were counted worthy to suffer dishonor for the name" (Acts 5:41). So, with these words, we are praying: may Your entire Person be held as holy by all.

"Thy Kingdom come." By this phrase, we are saying, Lord, may Your Kingdom soon be fully established in me and in the hearts of all, so that we might live together in Your peace and love. St. Francis of Assisi and his friars brought the joy and peace of God's Kingdom everywhere they went. In doing so, they rekindled the fire of God's love throughout Europe and beyond.

"Thy will be done on earth as it is in Heaven." This is a parallel phrase to the one just given. May we all do *and accept* Your will here on earth as it is done and accepted in Heaven. This is one of the most difficult phrases in the Our Father, and it should never be spoken lightly. It involves a surrender of our wills to God's will, be it pleasant or unpleasant. When we lose a loved one, it is hard to say, "Thy will be done." In fact, it is a barometer of our love of God to be able to say this sincerely in such a time of intense sadness. This is the cross Jesus promised us if we would follow Him. Mysteriously, our happiness is contained in the will of God; nowhere else.

What is God's will *for us*? That we become holy, "perfected," as Jesus said (see Matt. 5:48). We should keep that in mind when we pray the Our Father.

"Give us this day our daily bread." *Bread* here refers to our needs. We ask God to supply them as He does for the birds of the air and the flowers of the fields. And, if we pray this sincerely, we can be sure that God will indeed supply us with our true needs. The Fathers of the Church also saw this bread as referring to the Bread of Life, the Eucharist, the food for our souls.

"And forgive us our trespasses as we forgive those who trespass against us." Here again is a difficult thing to say. May You forgive our sins, Lord as we forgive others, even our enemies. In fact, this is the only passage in the Our Father upon which Jesus elaborates. He says "If you do not forgive [others] their trespasses, neither will your Father forgive your trespasses." (Matt. 6:15). Forgiveness is a central trait of a true Christian. When we think of the many sins God forgives us, it is a mere pittance for us to forgive even the most grievous injustices we have received. In fact, our chances of getting heart disease or cancer are considerably reduced if we forgive others.[64]

"And lead us not into temptation." That is, keep us not only from sin but from the very situation where sin is appealing. Anyone who truly loves another will not only avoid sinning against that person, but will stay far from the situation that has led to that sin. We pray to be delivered from temptation, but we must do our part to accept God's grace to avoid it. How many young men and women seek forgiveness for their sins of the flesh, yet go back to the same situations which have led to those sins.

"But deliver us from evil." That is, Lord, deliver us from the evil one. Let us never be under his spell in any way.

"Amen." Let it be so.

Notice, in this beautiful prayer, sometimes called the "perfect prayer," three of the four motives for prayer are exercised. Adoration is behind the words "hallowed be Thy name"; supplication, or petitions are found throughout the prayer (for example, "Give us

---

[64] See for example, Fred Luskin, *Forgive for Good: A Proven Prescription for Health and Happiness*, San Francisco: HarperCollins, 2002, pp. 78, 79.

this day our daily bread"); and, contrition is the motive for saying "forgive us our trespasses." We should often pray the Our Father and slowly meditate on the meaning of these beautiful words.

St. Teresa of Ávila wrote a long meditation on the Our Father and wrote at one point,

> To keep you from thinking that little is gained through a perfect recitation of vocal prayer, I tell you that it is very possible that while you are reciting the Our Father or some other vocal prayer, the Lord may raise you to perfect contemplation.[65]

CONVERSATION WITH GOD

The more we pray, the more comfortable we feel talking to God during our day. There should be scores of things each day that we thank God for, such as the weather, our own health, the blessing of food, our family and friends. Every good thing we experience should remind us to thank God. And, of course, we should feel comfortable asking God for what we need, adding the condition, "If it be for my good and according to your will."

Ours is a personal God. Jesus told us that God has counted every hair on our head (Luke 12:7). He cares about everything we do. If we have a personal relationship with God, we should feel comfortable speaking to Him all day long, knowing how close He is to us.

---

[65] St. Teresa of Ávila, *The Way of Perfection*, found in *The Collected Works of St. Teresa of Ávila*, vol. II, trans. by Keiran Kavanaugh, O.C.D. and Otilio Rodriguez, O.C.D., Washington, D.C.: ICS Publications, 1976, p. 131.

8

MEDITATION AND CONTEMPLATION

According to the *Catechism of the Catholic Church*, "Meditation is a prayerful quest engaging thought, imagination, emotion, and desire. Its goal is to make our own in faith the subject considered, by confronting it with the reality of our own life" (CCC 2723). To put it more simply, meditation is thinking in a focused way about something of God, especially an aspect in the life of Christ. Meditation is sometimes called *mental prayer*.

An example of meditation would be to read a passage of Scripture, and then close your eyes and reflect on it. You might try to find a lesson in it and apply it to your own life. This has traditionally been called *Lectio Divina*, literally *divine reading* (of Scripture, usually). It would involve reading the Scriptures or other classic spiritual works, such as the *Imitation of Christ*. I would recommend the Gospels as a wonderful source. You read until you come across something that catches your attention. (I do not recommend reading genealogies for this!)

Once you have chosen a text, you would ponder its meaning and perhaps apply it to your own life. After that, you open your heart to receive the message from God and embrace it in love and adoration. You seek to embrace the message intuitively. Finally, you allow yourself to rejoice in the gift of God's presence and consider a way in which you could apply this to your life and so grow in virtue.[66]

Other examples of meditation would be the Rosary, or the Stations of the Cross. In both cases, the meditations come from the Scriptures. Meditation is considered the highest form of active prayer (contemplation being more receptive than active), perhaps because it is a way of allowing God to speak to us through His Word or through the life of Christ. So often when we pray, we do all the talking, and God can hardly get a word in edgewise. When we meditate we listen to God and allow His words to sink deep into our subconscious. We should remember that God has given us only one mouth but two ears!

THE ROSARY

How is the Rosary a meditative prayer and not simply a multiplication of Hail Marys as some of our separated brethren believe? The Rosary is meant to be a meditation on the twenty mysteries with the ten Hail Marys being simply gentle background "music" to accompany the meditation and measure time. In fact, it is recommended, while praying a mystery, to think only about the mystery and not concentrate on the words of the Hail Mary at all. The recitation of the Rosary is the only time you would say a vocal prayer and not think about the words you are saying.

There are many advantages to praying the Rosary, including the following. The twenty mysteries of the Rosary focus on the central events of our Faith and are based on Sacred Scripture. Each mystery can be found either literally or figuratively in Scripture, and portrays

---

[66] This is based in part on Sam Anthony Morello, O.C.D., *Lectio Divina and the Practice of Teresian Prayer*, Washington, DC: ICS Publications, 1994, pp. 20–25; and Thomas Dubay, S.M. *Prayer Primer*, Cincinnati, OH: Servant Books, 2002, pp. 70, 71.

an important happening in the life of Jesus and His mother. Once the meditations are learned, through using Sacred Scripture as a guide or a booklet of meditations published for this purpose,[67] the Rosary can be said anywhere and anytime, while driving a car, in a crowded airport, or on a bus or train. For discretion or convenience, a rosary that fits on the finger like a ring may be used.

The Rosary can be said alone or in community with others since it is one of the few meditative prayers that lends itself easily to group prayer. The beads running through one's fingers are a psychological aid to concentration. It can be recited in three-minute segments since each decade takes about three minutes to say; it isnt necessary to say all five mysteries in one sitting. The mysteries may be spread out over the course of the day, which is an ideal way for introducing the prayer to young children or busy adults, who may think it too much to pray five mysteries all at once. Two or three mysteries a day makes a good beginning. Parents can use pictures and tell the story of each mystery to their children before and after praying. This makes prayer more interesting and provides a learning experience for the children as well. Children are often delighted with the stories of the mysteries and are eager to learn more.

Another advantage to the Rosary is that it contains the essential mysteries of our Faith, and thus leads us into the Mass which is the source and the summit of the Christian life. It includes the Apostle's Creed, the statement of our Faith, and the Our Father, the perfect prayer. The twenty different mysteries provide variety for meditation. Each decade is concluded with the "Glory be to the Father," in praise of the Blessed Trinity, and the Fatima prayer, "O my Jesus ..."

---

[67] Two such booklets on the Rosary by the author can be found at www.cfalive.com.

If your mind wanders off to some unrelated topic during private recitation of the Rosary, you may repeat some Hail Marys. This is a way to teach yourself the discipline of concentration. And, finally, the Rosary allows you to meditate at several different levels. You may simply meditate on the event of the mystery or on its basic theme, or on the virtue suggested by the event (some call this latter the *fruit* of the mystery).

Another way of meditating is one suggested by St. Louis de Montfort and Popes Paul VI and John Paul II, to add a descriptive phrase after the word *Jesus* in the Hail Mary. The following are based, in part, on St. Louis's suggestions:[68]

Joyful
1 – Jesus incarnate
2 – Jesus sanctifying
3 – Jesus born in poverty
4 – Jesus acclaimed
5 – Jesus lost and found

Luminous
1 – Jesus baptized
2 – Jesus Who worked a miracle at Cana
3 – Jesus Who proclaimed the Kingdom
4 – Jesus transfigured
5 – Jesus our Eucharist

---

[68] St. Louis de Montfort, *Methods for Saying the Rosary*, found in *God Alone: The Collected Writings of St. Louis Marie de Montfort*, Bayshore, NY: Montfort Publications, 1987, p. 237. For the papal recommendations, see Pope John Paul II's *Rosarium Virginis Mariae*, n. 33 and Paul VI's *Marialis Cultis*, n. 46.

Sorrowful
1 – Jesus in agony
2 – Jesus scourged
3 – Jesus crowned with thorns
4 – Jesus carrying His cross
5 – Jesus Crucified

Glorious
1 – Jesus risen from the dead
2 – Jesus ascending
3 – Jesus sending the Spirit
4 – Jesus assuming you up
5 – Jesus crowning you

Some of our Protestant brothers and sisters have come to appreciate the value of the Rosary. Richard Bauman, a German Lutheran minister, said this about the Rosary:

> In saying the rosary, truth sinks into the subconscious like a slow and heavy downpour. The hammered sentences of the Gospel receive an indelible validity for precisely the little ones, the least, to who[m belong] the Kingdom of Heaven … The Rosary is a long and persevering gaze, a meditation, a quieting of the spirit in the praise of God, the value of which we Protestants are learning more and more.[69]

According to *Soul* magazine in March–April 1990, the divorce rate for couples praying the Rosary together every day was one in five hundred—as compared to the national average of two in five. Thus, it is no wonder that Pope John Paul II wrote:

[69] "Prayer Index," from Rosary Workshop, found at http://www.rosary-workshop.com/PRAYERindex.htm.

We now desire, as a continuation of the thought of our predecessors, to recommend strongly the recitation of the family rosary.... There is no doubt that ... the rosary should be considered as one of the best and most efficacious prayers in common that the Christian family is invited to recite. We like to think and sincerely hope that when the family gathering becomes a time of prayer the rosary is a frequent and favored manner of praying.[70]

Pope John Paul II called the Rosary his favorite prayer, and he said at Fatima on May 12, 1980, "Would you like me to tell you a secret? It is simple, and after all, it is no secret. Pray, pray much. Pray the rosary every day."

Another pope, Benedict XV, wrote, "The prayer of the Rosary is perfect because of the praises it offers, the lessons it teaches, the graces it obtains, and the victories it achieves."[71] And, St. Charles Borromeo wrote, "The most divine prayer after the Mass and the sacraments is the rosary." St. Francis de Sales proclaimed, "The best method of prayer is the rosary."

Our Lady herself has told us of the importance of praying the Rosary. When she appeared at Fatima on May 13, 1917, she said to Lucia, Francisco, and Jacinta, "Pray the Rosary every day to obtain peace for the world, and the end of the war." On July 13, she reiterated, "Continue to say five decades of the Rosary every day in honor of Our Lady of The Rosary to obtain peace in the

---

[70] Pope John Paul II, *Familiaris Consortio* (On the Christian Family in the Modern World), November 22, 1981, n. 61, found at https://www.ewtn.com/catholicism/library/familiaris-consortio-on-the-family-8191. (This is a quote from Paul VI, *Marialis Cultus* (On Devotion to the Blessed Virgin Mary), February 2, 1974, nn. 52, 54.)

[71] Pope Benedict XV, "The Importance of the Meditated Holy Rosary," from The MGR Foundation, found at http://www.mgr.org/jp2rosary.html.

world and an end to the war. . . . If people do what I tell you, many souls will be saved and there will be peace."[72] Do we want world peace?

THE STATIONS OF THE CROSS[73]

Praying the Stations of the Cross is another way of meditating, on one of the most important subjects of meditation: the suffering and death of our Lord. Although the Stations are most often prayed on the Fridays of Lent, some pray them every day. Pope John Paul II used to pray them every day during Lent and every Friday throughout the year. Christ said to St. Maria Faustina, "There is more merit to one hour of meditation on the Sorrowful Passion than there is to a whole year of bloody scourging."[74]

CONTEMPLATION

The *Catechism* defines contemplation as follows:

> Contemplative prayer is the simple expression of the mystery of prayer. It is a gaze of faith fixed on Jesus, an attentiveness to the Word of God, a silent love. It achieves real union with the prayer of Christ to the extent that it makes us share in his mystery. (CCC 2724)

Fr. Thomas Dubay elaborates, "Christic contemplation is nothing less than a deep love communion with the triune God.... It is not

---

[72] William Thomas Walsh, *Our Lady of Fatima*, New York: Image Books, 1954, pp. 52, 80, 81.

[73] To see a booklet by the author on the Stations of the Cross go to www.cfalive.com.

[74] St. Maria Faustina, *Divine Mercy in My Soul: Diary of Saint Maria Faustina Kowalska*, Stockbridge, MA: Marian Press, 1990, n. 369, p. 166.

merely a mentally expressed 'I love You.' It is a wordless awareness and love that we of ourselves cannot initiate or prolong."[75]

We read in the First Letter of John: "Whoever confesses that Jesus is the Son of God, God abides in him, and he in God. So we know and believe the love God has for us. God is love, and he who abides in love abides in God, and God abides in him" (1 John 4:15–16). It is this mutual abiding or dwelling within each other that constitutes contemplative prayer.

This contemplative prayer is not something we can produce: it is entirely God's initiative. St. Teresa of Ávila said she could not produce the first "spark" of this fire of God's love that penetrated her. It was all His doing.[76] She pointed out that, although this prayer was filled with delight, this delight should not be something we seek here, but we should rather seek to share in the Cross of Christ.[77]

Fr. Dubay states that our life of virtue must grow if we wish to be able to grow in contemplation. If "humility, patience, temperance, chastity and love of neighbor are not growing, neither is prayer growing."[78] And, he adds that there are many different levels of contemplation.[79]

Thus, although this sort of prayer depends totally on the initiative of God, we can prepare ourselves for it. The purpose of this book is to help us prepare for this intimacy.

---

[75] Fr. Thomas Dubay, S.M., *Fire Within*, San Francisco: Ignatius Press, 1989, p. 57.

[76] St. Teresa of Ávila, *The Book of Her Life*, found in *The Collected Works of St. Teresa of Ávila*, p. 275.

[77] St. Teresa of Ávila, *The Book of Her Life*, found in *The Collected Works of St. Teresa of Ávila*, p. 148.

[78] Fr. Thomas Dubay, S.M., *Fire Within*, p. 59.

[79] Ibid., p. 60.

9

PRAISE AND WORSHIP

THE LITURGY OF THE HOURS

WHEN WE THINK of the prayer of praise, we should think of the Psalms. Priests and religious are required to pray a number of the psalms daily in the Liturgy of the Hours, otherwise known as the Divine Office or the breviary. There are five parts for this prayer, plus two additional parts for members of contemplative orders. The five parts are as follows:

1. Office of Readings—three psalms, a Scripture reading, and a reading by or about a saint. This may be said the evening before or any time during the day of prayer.

2. Morning Prayer (Lauds)—three psalms, a reading, response, a Gospel Canticle (the Benedictus prayer, i.e., the Canticle of Zechariah upon discovering that Elizabeth was with child), petitions, the Our Father, and a closing prayer.

3. Daytime Prayer—three psalms, a short reading, a brief response, and a closing prayer. This is said around noon. If three parts are said, it is said at 9:00 a.m., noon, and 3:00 p.m.

4. Evening Prayer (Vespers)—same format as Morning Prayer except that the Gospel Canticle is the Magnificat (the humble prayer of Mary upon visiting Elizabeth).

5. Night Prayer (Compline)—usually one psalm with a response, a short reading, a Gospel Canticle (the prayer of Simeon upon seeing the Christ-child at the presentation), a closing prayer, and a hymn or prayer to Mary.

You need not pray the Divine Office to pray the Psalms, but it is the official prayer of the Church; using this means that you are praying with the whole Church.

THE PSALMS

The Psalms are a beautiful way of praising God using the songs that were sung in the Jewish liturgy. These are the songs Christ would have sung. They speak of the greatness of God, His mercy, His fidelity, His power, His goodness, His knowledge of all things, past, present, and future, His justice, His love for us, how small we are in comparison, and yet how He has given us great dignity and power. They tell us how to be happy by following God's way, of our need to call on God in difficult times, that crime does not pay, that God will answer our prayers for help, that He is worthy of complete trust, that He is always near to us and concerned for us. Reading the Psalms should remind us how special we are because of the dignity God has given us—Psalm 8, for example, is about the concern this magnificent God has for us, making us little less than a god. The Psalms tell us that God's law is good and shows us the way to happiness, that He is our shepherd, and that He guides us through life toward His Kingdom.

Anyone who prays the Psalms regularly will certainly know Who God is, and who we are. This is especially helpful for people who have had difficult fathers and need to discover a completely different understanding of our God as Father. It is here in the Psalms that we discover the true Father and the proper meaning of fatherhood.

PRAISING GOD

The Psalms are a wonderful instrument to praise God, which is the prayer of adoration. However, there is another way to praise God, which can be a day-long outpouring of love and joy in the Lord. This is to praise God for everything that happens in your life, good or bad. Especially the bad.

Why? Because, as Merlin Carothers pointed out in his book, *Prison to Praise*, Romans 8 tells us "We know that in everything God works for good with those who love him" (Rom. 8:28). If we love God we can be sure that whatever happens will somehow be for our good. To praise God even for the apparently bad things that happen is to trust Him, and God loves trust. He told St. Maria Faustina:

> The graces of my mercy are drawn by means of one vessel only, and that is trust. The more a soul trusts, the more it will receive. Souls that trust boundlessly are a great comfort to me, because I pour all the treasures of my grace into them.[80]

He also told her, "Sins of distrust wound me most painfully."[81]

---

[80] Sr. Sophia Michalenko, *Mercy My Mission: Life of Sister Faustina H. Kowalska*, Stockbridge, MA: Marian Press, 1987, p. 215.

[81] St. Maria Faustina, *Divine Mercy in My Soul: Diary of Saint Maria Faustina Kowalska*, n. 1076, p. 404.

10

DIFFICULTIES IN PRAYER

SOME PEOPLE CLAIM that they have so many distractions in prayer, they get discouraged. Some say prayer is just too boring. Others lose heart when the good feelings, the "consolations" they used to get disappear. Still others have told me, "I don't have time for prayer. I am too busy." Not to worry. There's a solution for each of these.

IS PRAYER BORING?

Is prayer boring? Of course, it's boring—at first. Many things are boring at first. Take school for starters. That can be extremely boring. However, as time goes on and we begin to develop a base of knowledge, it becomes more interesting, but it's very boring at first. Most people persevere in studying because they want to become educated or they want to get a well-paying job.

Sports can also be boring in the early stages. When I went out for the track team in high school, all we did was exercises for the first two weeks. Only after that did I get to do what I came for, high-jumping and pole-vaulting. Football is the same. No football for several weeks in training camp: weeks of boring, hard workouts in college or pro football. They lift weights all during the off-season. That too is boring.

Most jobs are boring at first. We persevere because we are getting paid.

Suppose we decided to just do things that were stimulating—no more boring activities. No school, no organized sports, no chores at home, no jobs. Just lots of television watching, computer games, and other games. We'd end up in jail! Think of all the things in life that have made you a better person. Studying, training for sports, helping others, doing work. All boring at first, but all enriching.

So is prayer—early on. Were we expecting a party to get to the Kingdom? Isn't it interesting that we are willing to endure some boredom to get an education, to work at a job and earn money, to train for a sports team? For money or for sports we are willing to accept some boredom, but to thank God for creating and sustaining us, for giving us every good thing simply so He could share with us His happiness, some of us shun boredom. Sunday Mass? Prayer? Too boring!

Jesus Himself promised a cross for those who would follow Him. He said, "If any man would come after me, let him deny himself take up his cross daily and follow me. For whoever would save his life will lose it; and whoever loses his life for my sake, he will save it" (Luke 9:23–24). Some apparently think that boredom mustn't be included in that cross. But boredom at prayer or worship is indeed, often the first cross of a Christian.

St. Teresa of Ávila was extremely bored by prayer. She felt so miserable when it was time to enter the chapel for meditative prayer that she had to force herself to go in to pray. She could hardly wait for the hour to be up. Nonetheless, after she made herself do this, she often felt better about the prayer she had done than when she felt like praying![82] Later, Teresa wrote of prayer that when she abandoned prayer it was as though she were "putting myself right in hell without the need of devils."[83] She also wrote, "There is but one road

---

[82] St. Teresa of Ávila, *The Book of Her Life*, found in *The Collected Works of St. Teresa of Ávila*, vol. I, p. 68.

[83] St. Teresa of Ávila, *The Book of Her Life*, found in *The Collected Works of St. Teresa of Ávila*, vol. I, p. 124.

which reaches God and that is prayer; if anyone shows you another, you are being deceived." This transformation of Teresa is typical of many who begin to pray—it is extremely difficult at first to get into the habit, but once a person has gotten through that difficulty, they begin to love prayer, especially when they see what it does for them.

DISTRACTIONS

Should we worry about distractions in prayer? No. Everyone has distractions, even the saints. St. Thérèse explained to a novice what she did when distracted in prayer: "I also have many [distractions] but as soon as I am aware of them I pray for those people the thought of whom is diverting my attention. In this way they reap the benefit of my distractions."

According to a legend told by Bishop Sheen, St. Bernard was out riding with a friend once and lamented his distractions in prayer. His friend remarked that he was never distracted in prayer. Bernard said he found that hard to believe and offered to give his friend the horse he was riding if the friend could stop right there, kneel down, and say one Our Father without a single distraction.

His companion accepted the challenge. He dismounted, knelt down and began to pray out loud. When he got to the words "give us this day our daily bread" he stopped, looked up at St. Bernard, and asked: "Do I get the saddle too?" St. Bernard kept his horse!

We should not be surprised if we are distracted at prayer. When we have distractions, as soon as we become aware of them, we need only bring our minds back to God and try again to keep them focused on the subject of our meditation or on our prayer. When praying the Rosary, we may avoid distractions by using one of the booklets on the Rosary,[84] which contain meditations on each mystery. Or, if riding in a car, we might play a recording of meditations

---

[84] See two by this author at www.cfalive.com.

on the Rosary. There are several of these available online; search the Internet for "Rosary recordings."

St. Teresa of Ávila found herself very distracted one day after receiving Holy Communion. She began to envy those living in the desert without any distractions. She heard the voice of the Lord, "You are greatly mistaken, daughter; rather the temptations of the devil there are stronger; be patient, for as long as you live, a wandering mind cannot be avoided."[85]

CONSOLATIONS

How often, too, people say to me they don't think they are praying as effectively as they ought. I try to remind them of the words of St. Teresa of Ávila who told us: "The Lord does not look so much at the magnitude of anything we do as at the love with which we do it."[86] God measures effort more than results. St. Francis de Sales wrote, "We should labor, therefore, without any uneasiness as to results. God requires efforts on our part, but not success."[87]

Some people say their prayer doesn't seem to "go anywhere." They don't get that wonderful feeling they used to get in prayer. This should never worry us. At times we all have what is called *dryness* in prayer, or prayer with no consolations. Unfortunately, some individuals withdraw from prayer when this happens. But this is wrong. We should pray all the harder when everything is "dry," knowing that we receive that much more grace when prayer is dry. As St. Francis de Sales wrote

---

[85] St. Teresa of Ávila, *Spiritual Testimonies*, found in *The Collected Works of St. Teresa of Ávila*, vol. I, p. 341.

[86] St. Teresa of Ávila, *Interior Castle*, found in *The Collected Works of St. Teresa of Ávila*, vol. II, p. 350.

[87] Found in R. P. Quadrupani, *Light and Peace: Instructions for Devout Souls to Dispel Their Doubts and Allay Their Fears*, Rockford, IL: TAN Books, 1980, p. 51.

regarding prayer: "If [God] consoles me, I kiss the right hand of His mercy; If I am dry and distracted, I kiss the left hand of His justice."[88] And St. Thérèse, the Little Flower, said: "My claim to Heaven will be, I prayed in the darkness when all was dry."

Why does God permit us to suffer dryness in prayer? Why doesn't He reward us with consolations every time we pray? Because, by withdrawing the consolations, God is asking us: "Do you love Me, or My consolations?" He wants to see if we will love Him as spouses promise to love, in good times and in bad. St. Francis de Sales tells us to seek not the consolations of God, but the God of all consolations.

COMMUNITY PRAYER

Is it better to pray alone, or with others, as a group? Our natural inclination may be to pray alone, but the Lord encouraged us to pray with others: "For where two or three are gathered in my name, there am I in the midst of them" (Matt. 18:20). St. John Vianney said:

> Private prayer resembles straw scattered here and there over a field; if it is set on fire, the flame is not a powerful one; but if you gather those scattered straws into a bundle, the flame is bright and rises in a lofty column towards the sky: such is public prayer.[89]

Perhaps we have all thought, as I have, "I could pray the Rosary much faster saying it alone than saying it with the parishioners after Mass." However, we must remember that, although it takes more time, we receive far more grace by saying it with others. Even if it

---

[88] Found in R. P. Quadrupani, *Light and Peace: Instructions for Devout Souls to Dispel Their Doubts and Allay Their Fears*, p. 23.

[89] Abbé Francis Trochu, *The Curé d'Ars: St. Jean-Marie Baptiste Vianney*, p. 310.

took twice as long, it would be worth it, since we might speculate that it could be three or four times as beneficial.

ANSWERED PRAYERS?

Often when we pray for a specific favor from the Lord, we fail to notice that He has answered us. The story is told of the man who was looking for a parking space, already late for an important meeting. He prayed, "Lord, if You find me a space, I will pray the Rosary every day." Alas, no space was forthcoming. He prayed further, "Lord, if You find me a space, I will give up drinking." Immediately someone pulled out, and he got his space. He said, "Never mind, Lord. I found a space myself."

Another story tells of a man who stayed with his house during a flood. As the waters rose, he climbed to the top of his roof. With the water swirling around, a rowboat came by and offered him a ride to safety. He told the rowers, "No, thanks. I have prayed to God, and He will save me." Shortly thereafter, as the waters continued to rise and his space on the roof shrank a motor boat offered him a saving ride, but his reply was the same. Finally, as he clung to the top of the chimney a helicopter offered him a rope to climb up to safety but again he declined, saying, "God will save me." Finally, he was swept away in the flood waters, and he drowned. When he met the Lord, he complained, "Lord, You disappointed me. I prayed that You would save me, and I ended up drowning. What happened?" The Lord answered him, "I sent three different people to save you, and you turned them all down."

How important it is to realize that the way God answers our prayers is often by sending someone to give us what we need. And how important that we see that, and thank Him!

COMMITMENT TO PRAYER

HOW MUCH TIME should we spend each day in prayer? Naturally, this depends on our age, our state in life, and a number of other factors, but perhaps we might try to establish some averages. For someone leading a busy life who has never prayed more than two or three short prayers at morning and night, I usually recommend a commitment of at least five minutes a day of meditation. That's not much time, but to do this amount of prayer each day for several months is to begin in the way of holiness, the way to the Kigdom. Anyone who claims to be too busy for this has no concept of what he or she owes God in gratitude for all His gifts and is asking for trouble — eternal trouble.

St. Teresa of Ávila wrote, "It is essential to begin the practice of prayer with a firm resolution of persevering in it." It's easier to go from five minutes a day to fifteen minutes a day than to go from a couple of short prayers to five minutes of meditation daily. Anyone who prays comes to realize that, as St. John Vianney said, "The more we pray, the more we wish to pray."[90] Of course, the opposite is true as well: the less you pray, the less you want to pray. As we continue to pray, no matter how hard we find it at first, the easier

---

[90] Jill Haak Adels, *The Wisdom of the Saints: An Anthology*, Oxford: Oxford University Press, 1989, p. 40.

it becomes. Perhaps the great miracle in anyone's life is their first commitment to pray.

GETTING STARTED

Beginning to pray is often a great trial for modern man. We are so busy making money, studying, having fun that we find it difficult to stop all that and quiet down our senses, and pray to God in silence. We can't see God, we can't touch Him, we can't hear Him the way we hear others, and we're not sure He hears us or answers us. And yet, we must communicate with Him to fulfill His greatest commandment, to love Him. As noted earlier, St. Alphonsus Liguori said: "Those who pray are certainly saved; those who do not pray are certainly damned."[91]

So, to begin this communication is of utmost importance. We need not be elegant about it or follow any defined structures at first. We don't have to pray before the Blessed Sacrament, even though that is the best place to pray, and we don't have to pray on our knees at first.

I began to pray in bed at night, and because it often took a half hour for me to get to sleep, I usually finished praying five Mysteries of the Rosary nightly. That was my first commitment to pray and to that foundation I attribute every good thing that followed in my life. My mother used to say that if I fell asleep before finishing the Rosary, my angel would finish it for me. That's not dogma, but I am willing to bet that it's true.

Imagine if we could get every person to use all the time while waiting to fall asleep for prayer. What a beautiful world we would have! So much time is wasted. What else can we do during this time?

---

[91] St. Alphonsus Liguori, *Del gran Mezzo della preghiera*, found in CCC 2744.

Perhaps we can ponder our work problems, or how we might win the heart of a new love, but most people just waste this time. In fact, thinking about work or one's love life tends to keep us awake, while praying tends to quiet us better for sleep. Some count sheep to help them sleep. How much better to pray to the Lamb!

One mother told her daughter not to pray in bed. She felt it wasn't respectful to fall asleep while communicating with the Lord. But look at it this way: how beautiful it is to share our final words and thoughts each day with our Lord. And, how beautiful to spend fifteen minutes or more each day in prayer to God, which we might not otherwise spend with Him.

What a great way to encourage people to pray, especially those who think they're too busy to pray. I often poll young people on how long it takes them to fall asleep, and invariably a large majority raise their hands when I ask how many take fifteen or more minutes to get to sleep.

Now what about those who fall asleep within minutes of hitting the pillow? What a blessing. Had I had such a gift, I would willingly kneel by the bed and pray fifteen minutes a night, *at least*, in gratitude.

Young mothers can pray as they rest in bed while their children take a nap in the afternoon. Or they can pray out loud with their children who are too young to understand prayer. Many people pray while they are driving or walking. Some pray while they are waiting in line at the grocery store. My mother used to pray during the commercials while watching television.

Isn't that disrespectful, watching television while praying? Yes, of course. There's a story of two religious discussing whether they should pray at the same time they watched television. They couldn't agree on an answer, so they wrote to Rome for an answer. The first wrote asking if it was okay to watch television while praying, and the answer came back, "Absolutely not." The second wrote asking if it was okay to pray while watching television. The answer he got was, "Yes, that's fine."

Sure, dedicated prayer on your knees before the Blessed Sacrament is best, but you needn't start with that. Sure, it's better to pray the Sorrowful Mysteries of the Rosary on Tuesday and Friday, on rosary beads, but if you don't know which days to do which mysteries, and you don't have rosary beads handy, pray any mystery you know, and use your fingers. Start doing the best you can and later on you can refine things. Don't let anything stop you from getting into prayer.

GROWING IN PRAYER

Once a person has made a daily habit of prayer, he or she ought to begin to slowly increase the time spent in prayer. Many have discovered that the more generous they are with God in prayer, the more efficient He will make them in their work. Thus, we lose nothing by making more time for the Lord in prayer. St. (Mother) Teresa of Calcutta used to say that, if we pray, we can do twice as much in less time because *we* are not doing it. God is.

Our growth in prayer should be steady, not advancing too quickly so as to become burdensome, and not settling into a rut in which we stagnate at a certain level. Bishop Fulton Sheen used to say in his retreats that there are no plains in the spiritual life. We are either going uphill, or we are going down. If we are doing the same now as we were last year, we are worse, for the spiritual life was meant to grow.

How do we know if we are praying enough? I believe our prayers should make us be a bit uncomfortable, but not burdened. If we find it comfortable, we are probably not praying enough. If we feel burdened by our prayer commitment, we are probably trying to grow too quickly. It is impossible to become a saint overnight. If we find it easy to complete our prayer commitment, it's probably time to grow.

Prayer is like lifting weights. If you go into the weight room and put one small weight on the bar and keep lifting that, you will never get strong. If, on the other hand you put too much weight on the bar, you may hurt yourself, or you may become quite discouraged and give up. But, if you do things properly, you will start with a weight which challenges you, something you can lift, but not too easily. As you get stronger, you add more weight every few weeks, and you keep getting stronger. As you grow in prayer, your relationship with God keeps getting stronger, and you are better able to overcome sin and become holy and virtuous.

In terms of time, what sort of goal should we have for prayer? Although we don't find the answer directly in Scripture, I think it's there indirectly. In the Old Testament, we find over and over the Israelites giving one tenth of their goods to the Lord. Abraham gave a tenth of everything to Melchizedek, the priest of God Most High, who was a Christ figure (Gen. 14:18–20). The Lord commanded the Israelites to tithe, giving 10 percent of their goods to the Levites as a contribution to the Lord who were in turn to give 10 percent of what they received to the Lord (Num. 18:21–24). If they gave 10 percent of their goods, could we not give 10 percent of both our goods and our time to the Lord? Ten percent of our waking hours for most of us is a little more than an hour and a half each day.

THE HABIT OF PRAYER

When I was a young boy, I was convinced there was only one kind of habit—bad. That was the only type I seemed to have. Then, after fourteen cavities and many unpleasant visits to the dentist, I developed my first good habit: brushing my teeth. From that tender age, I began to brush my teeth daily, and never gave it another thought. I never asked myself if I were going to brush my teeth, I just did it.

So it should be with prayer. We should develop a habit of prayer, such that we just do it each day, without question.

Granted, because of schedule changes, we may have to move our prayer time here and there during the day, but, if we consider it a priority, we will rearrange our schedule to make sure we do it. The things we really want to get done, we schedule as early as possible in the day. This is not to say we won't pray late in the day, but most of our prayer should be done before 9:00 p.m., so that we are wide awake and give God our best hours. For many, this might mean right after dinner.

Isn't this a contradiction to what we already said about praying in bed? No, because praying in bed is meant as an incentive for those who are just beginning prayer, and who might think themselves too busy to set aside time for it during the day. If our commitment is just fifteen minutes a day of prayer, praying in bed might cover it. However, when we begin to pray half an hour daily, and more, much of that should be done long before bedtime. We should never give God just the dregs of our day. Of course, we should pray before we retire for the night, but that need only be something brief—such as an Examination of Conscience and an Act of Contrition—if we have prayed a good deal during the day.

THE IMPORTANCE OF PRAYER

St. Alphonsus Ligouri said, "Prayer is a necessary means of salvation without which we cannot remain in the grace of God. The damned have been damned because they did not pray; the saints have become saints because they did pray."[92] Prayer is our most fundamental way of loving God; without it, we lose our very connection with God,

[92] St. Alphonsus Liguori, *To Serve Christ Jesus: Selected Writings on the Spiritual Life*, Immaculata, PA: Servants of the Immaculate Heart of Mary, 1974, p. 51.

our faith will die, and our soul will shrivel up like a dead flower. With prayer, we blossom day after day with the very life of God. We can show God to the world!

We read in First Thessalonians: "Rejoice always, pray constantly, give thanks in all circumstances; for this is the will of God in Christ Jesus for you" (1 Thess. 5:16–18). Jesus told the disciples the parable of the corrupt judge, who cared little about justice, but responded to the widow's pleas because she was so persistent. He promised that God would answer those who "cry to him day and night" (Luke 18:7). The point of it was "that they ought always to pray and not lose heart" (Luke 18:1). Our Blessed Lord told Peter, the night He was betrayed, "Watch and pray that you may not enter into temptation" (Matt 26:41). Bishop Sheen commented that, after having denied Christ three times, and enduring such anguish over betraying his beloved Lord, Peter must have wished that he had "watched and prayed."

The word *pray* appears seventy-two times in the Old Testament and seventy-six times in the New. The word *prayer* appears 197 times in the Old Testament, 126 in the New. The word *prayed* appears sixty-four times in the Old Testament and twenty times in the New.

The Gospel of Luke is known as the Gospel of Prayer. He often shows Jesus praying at key times in His life: at His baptism (3:21); before He chose the apostles (6:12); before Peter declared Him to be the Christ (9:18); before the Transfiguration (9:28); when He taught the disciples to pray (11:1); at the Last Supper (22:32); the night before He died (22:41); and finally, on the Cross (23:46). Luke also tells us Jesus would go off to quiet places to pray (5:16), and He warned the apostles to "keep watch" and pray to meet trials and "stand before" Him. Prayer should be in our blood!

St. Ignatius was always at prayer; St. Francis of Assisi spent long hours praying; it was during one of his extended periods of prayer that he received the stigmata. When St. Clare and St. John of the Cross came from prayer their faces glowed. St. John of the Cross wrote, "Do not omit mental prayer for any occupation, for it is the sustenance of your soul."[93] And, Fr. Henri Nouwen wrote that reminding people to pray was like reminding them to breathe!

To those who tell me they have a great deal of trouble getting into prayer, I suggest simply thanking God all day long for the good things in their lives. Those who have done so often begin, in time, to pray more formally. Another approach that has brought success is to invite a person to start with one Hail Mary daily, asking Mary to help them grow in time.

SHOW UP!

There are times when we feel we can't pray well, or we are upset about things, or we just have a bad attitude toward our prayer. It is important to remember that we receive grace for "showing up," for being there, whether we like it or not. We will never know how much grace we receive for being present for prayer, even if our hearts are far away. How many souls have been saved by persons of prayer just showing up for prayer, for Mass, for Confession, for anything done for God, when they would rather not. Better to run with joy to pray before our Lord and King, but if we cannot, let us at least be there for Him. If He rewards a cup of cold water given to His disciple (Matt. 10:42), how pleased He will be with our presence, regardless of our zeal or lack thereof. This perseverance is essential to strive for the holiness we need to live in the Kingdom.

---

[93] Found in Suzanne Clores, ed., *The Wisdom of the Saints*, New York: Citadel Press, 2002, p. 115.

12

SIN AND CONFESSION

A YOUNG MAN once gave a talk about his conversion. He had been a Catholic since childhood, but fell into sin and neglected Confession, though he continued to go to Mass. So, he did need a conversion. He went to confess one Saturday afternoon, and he found himself at the end of a long line of people. He looked at his watch and decided he didn't have time to go, so he started to leave, a bit relieved that he could put this Confession off some more. A woman close to the confessional grabbed him as he went by and said, "Here, take my place. You look like you may need it more that I." Indeed he did. He was caught—by the "Hound of Heaven"! He went in, confessed, and returned to the sacraments for the first time in over ten years. He went on to become a very good priest.

The point of this story is that his whole conversion story was centered on one event: his going to Confession after many, many years. This was the key to his changing his life and surrendering to God.

So often, Confession is the beginning of a great conversion. Bishop Sheen told the story of Charles de Foucauld, who had some questions about the Faith. He was directed to a Fr. Huvelin who was in the confessional at the time. He said, "Father, please come out. I want to ask you some questions." The priest answered, "No, you come in. I want to talk to you about your sins." After some back and forth discussion, Charles did what the priest had asked. That was the day de Foucald converted. He was later ordained a priest and became a hermit in the Sahara desert. He was beatified in 2005 by Pope Benedict XVI.

FREQUENT CONFESSION

There is a vast difference spiritually between those who go to Confession regularly—once a month or so—and those who do not. Confession has a way of making us more honest about ourselves and our relationship with God. A man once went on retreat and, when he told the retreat director in Confession that he hadn't confessed in several years, the priest warned him of the danger of this. He had no mortal sins, but he urged him to go frequently nonetheless, suggesting that it could be pride that was keeping him away. He resolved that day to start going regularly.

Although it is necessary to go to Confession for mortal sins, it important to go for just venial sins. Pope John Paul II taught:

> Though the Church knows and teaches that venial sins are forgiven in other ways too ... she does not cease to remind everyone of the special usefulness of the sacramental moment for these sins too. The frequent use of the Sacrament ... strengthens the awareness that even minor sins offend God and harm the Church, the Body of Christ.[94]

When we confess just venial sins, we develop a greater sensitivity to them, and become more inclined and strengthened to overcome them. Most people who commit mortal sins began with repeated venial sins, and, thus weakened, fell into more serious sins.

We *need* Confession to grow in our relationship with the Lord. Pius XII taught:

> To ensure more rapid progress day by day in the path of virtue, We will that the pious practice of frequent confession ... should be earnestly advocated. By it genuine self-knowledge is

[94] Pope John Paul II, *Reconciliatio et Paenitentia* (On Reconciliation and Penance), December 2, 1984, n. 32, found at https://www.ewtn.com/catholicism/library/on-reconciliation-and-penance-8387.

increased, Christian humility grows, bad habits are corrected, spiritual neglect and tepidity are resisted, the conscience is purified, the will strengthened, a salutary self-control is attained, and grace is increased in virtue of the Sacrament itself.[95]

CONFESSION BRINGS GREAT GRACE

We get a great deal of grace from this sacrament, and we grow in virtue as well. St. Francis de Sales wrote:

In confession you not only receive absolution from the . . . sins you confess, but also great strength to avoid them in the future, light to see them clearly, and abundant grace to repair whatever damage you have incurred. You will also practice the virtues of humility, obedience, simplicity, and charity. In the single act of confession you will exercise more virtues than in any other act whatsoever.[96]

St. John Vianney taught, "When you go to confession you must understand . . . you are about to un-nail Our Lord."[97]

KNOWLEDGE OF SINS

Whenever we meditate on the First Luminous Mystery, we should ask for the grace to know all our sins as did the people who came for John's baptism in the Jordan. And, we should ask that God reveal our sins gradually, so we will not be devastated by seeing them all at once!

---

[95] Pius XII, *Mystici Corporis Christi* (On the Mystical Body of Christ), June 29, 1943, n. 88, found at https://www.vatican.va/content/pius-xii/en/encyclicals/documents/hf_p-xii_enc_29061943_mystici-corporis-christi.html.

[96] St. Francis de Sales, *Introduction to the Devout Life*, trans. by John K. Ryan, New York: Image Books, 1972, part 2, chapter 19.

[97] George William Rutler, *Saint John Vianney: The Curé D'Ars Today*, San Francisco: Ignatius Press, 1988, p. 153.

We will surely never become holy if we don't develop a healthy sense of the horror of sin and a deep sense of sorrow for our sins. St. Dorotheus said, "It does not matter how many virtues a man may have, even if they are beyond number and limit. If he has turned from the path of self-accusation, he will never find peace."[98]

One way to stay focused on overcoming sin is to make a list of our three worst sins and examine it every night before retiring, and again upon awakening. It could be fewer than three, but never more, since it is hard to focus on more than three sins at a time; sharp focus is what we need to truly reform. By seeing this small list each night and morning on paper, we will be developing a deep awareness of our faults, and will be more ready to correct them.

One of the goals of doing this is to come to a point where we can, in time, delete one of the items on the list, and replace it with a lesser sin. And, certainly one of the benefits of this is that, with these three things in mind, it is usually very easy to examine our conscience in preparation for Confession.

The closer we get to God, the more we realize how far we are from Him. This is because, as St. John of the Cross wrote, when very bright sunlight shines in our room, we are able to see all the particles of dust in the air. So it is with intimacy with God: the closer we get to Him, the more clearly we see our sins, and the more we want them wiped clean.

Pope John Paul II went to Confession weekly, as did St. Dominic Savio. Sts. Thomas Aquinas, Margaret of Cortona, and Bridget of Sweden went to Confession just about every day. For anyone who is not prevented from going by external circumstances, frequent Confession—at least once a month—is an essential part of holiness.

---

[98] From Office of Readings, Monday, 9th Week of Ordinary Time, Week I, found at http://www.liturgies.net/Liturgies/Catholic/loh/week9mondayor.htm.

13

THE MASS: "SOURCE AND SUMMIT OF THE CHRISTIAN LIFE"[99]

The sacrifice of Christ and the sacrifice of the Eucharist are *one single sacrifice*: "The victim is one and the same: the same now offers through the ministry of priests, who then offered himself on the cross; only the manner of offering is different." "And since in this divine sacrifice which is celebrated in the Mass, the same Christ who offered himself once in a bloody manner on the altar of the cross is contained and is offered in an unbloody manner.... this sacrifice is truly propitiatory" (CCC 1367; quote from the Council of Trent.)

A SACRIFICE

Pope John Paul II taught, "The Eucharist is above all else a sacrifice."[100] And, it is more: "The Mass is at the same time, and inseparably, the sacrificial memorial in which the sacrifice of the cross is perpetuated and the sacred banquet of communion with the Lord's body and blood" (CCC 1382).

[99] See Vatican II, *Lumen Gentium*, n. 11.
[100] Pope John Paul II, *Dominicae Cenae* (On the Mystery and Worship of the Eucharist), February 24, 1980, n. 9, found at https://www.vatican.va/content/john-paul-ii/en/letters/1980/documents/hf_jp-ii_let_19800224_dominicae-cenae.html.

So, the Mass is, above all, the re-presentation of the one Sacrifice of Jesus' death on the Cross. And, it is also a sacred banquet of communion with our eucharistic Lord. It is the fulfillment of all the Old Testament sacrifices:

[The Mass] is, finally, that [sacrifice] which was prefigured by various types of sacrifices during the period of nature and of the law, which, namely, comprises all the good things signified by them, as being the consummation and perfection of them all.[101]

The "period of nature" is that time before the reception of the Ten Commandments; that of the law, the period after the law was given until Christ. So, the sacrificial lambs, the bulls, the goats, and the scapegoat in particular—were all foreshadowings of the true Sacrifice of Jesus Christ on the Cross. Those sacrifices had no power in and of themselves to remit sins, but, insofar as they were related to the true Sacrifice of Jesus, they did have that power.

THE REAL PRESENCE

Of course, for the Mass to truly be the re-offering of the Sacrifice of Jesus' death on Calvary, He would have to be truly present in the eucharistic species. And, He is. Jesus said:

Truly, truly, I say to you, unless you eat the flesh of the Son of man and drink his blood, you have no life in you; he who eats my flesh and drinks my blood has eternal life, and I will raise him up at the last day. For my flesh is food indeed, and

[101] Council of Trent, Session 22, September 17, 1562, Doctrine Concerning the Sacrifice of the Mass, chapter 1, found at https://www.ewtn.com/catholicism/library/twentysecond-session-of-the-council-of-trent-1489.

my blood is drink indeed. He who eats my flesh and drinks my blood abides in me, and I in him. (John 6:53–56)

Right from the first century, the Church has taken that literally, that the substance of bread and wine is changed miraculously into the substance of Jesus' Body and Blood. The *accidents*—that is, the appearance, taste, shape, and so forth—remain that of bread and wine but the substance (i.e., what it is) has changed into something different. When the Protestants doubted the Real Presence of Christ in the Eucharist in the sixteenth century, the Council of Trent made clear the Church's position:

> If anyone denies that in the sacrament of the most Holy Eucharist are contained truly, really and substantially the body and blood together with the soul and divinity of our Lord Jesus Christ, and consequently the whole Christ, but says that He is in it only as in a sign, or figure or force, let him be anathema.[102]

There have been a good number of miracles over the centuries that have confirmed the Real Presence of Jesus in the Eucharist. One involved a monk in Lanciano, Italy, in the eighth century, who doubted the Real Presence as he said Mass one day. Then, just after the Consecration, he noticed that the host had been transformed into a circle of flesh, and the wine was changed into visible blood. As he began to weep with joy he announced to the congregation:

> Oh fortunate witnesses to whom the Blessed God, to confound my unbelief, has wished to reveal Himself visible to

---

[102] Council of Trent, Session 13, October 11, 1551, Canons on the Most Holy Sacrament of the Eucharist, can. 1, found at https://www.ewtn.com/catholicism/library/thirteenth-session-of-the-council-of-trent-1479.

our eyes! Come, brethren, and marvel at our God, so close to us. Behold the flesh and blood of our most Beloved Christ.[103]

The congregation quickly came forward to see the miracle and after Mass, they went out to spread the news. Over the centuries many scientific tests have been made on these elements. In one such investigation it was discovered that the flesh was muscle tissue from the myocardium, that is the wall of the heart, and contained no trace of a preservative. The flesh and the blood were also shown to be of human origin, with the blood matching the blood type in the flesh. These miraculous relics can still be seen in the church now dedicated to St. Francis of Assisi in Lanciano, Italy.[104]

There have been over thirty such miracles, reassurances from God that the Eucharist is truly the Body and Blood of Christ.

SACRED BANQUET

As a "sacred banquet" of communion, the Mass was prefigured by several sacred meals:

- the life-saving meal offered as hospitality to one who was encountered in the desert by nomads;
- the joyful feast celebrating the covenant renewal with God;
- the Passover meal celebrating the Jews passing over from their slavery in Egypt to the Promised Land and God's passing over the Israelites when He struck down all the first-born of the Egyptians; and
- the feast of the unleavened bread, when the Jews celebrated new beginnings at the time of the wheat harvest

[103] Joan Carroll Cruz, *Eucharistic Miracles and Eucharistic Phenomena in the Lives of the Saints*, Rockford, IL: TAN Books, 1987, p. 3.
[104] Ibid., pp. 3–7.

in the spring—the leaven (a part of the previous bread-making dough) was used up and unleavened bread was eaten for a week before the people returned to eating (yeast-aided) leavened bread.

In the Mass, we celebrate our passing over from the slavery of sin and death to the new life of the final Promised Land: God's Kingdom of grace and love. This passing over was made possible by the saving event of Christ's death on the Cross. In the Mass, we offer the Lamb of God, Jesus, and then partake in this eucharistic feast as a sign of our covenant renewal with the Lord. This new covenant is Christ and His law of love. What a rich background the Mass has!

THE GLORY OF THE MASS

From the liturgy ... especially from the eucharist, as from a font, grace is poured forth upon us; and the sanctification of men in Christ and the glorification of God to which all other activities of the Church are directed as toward their end, is achieved in the most efficacious possible way.[105]

In other words, nothing we might do, no prayer we might offer, could ever equal the superabundant power of the Mass. St. Bernard of Clairvaux wrote, "One merits more by devoutly attending a Holy Mass than by distributing all his goods to the poor and traveling all over the world on pilgrimage."[106] St. Francis de Sales wrote:

[105] Vatican II, *Sacrosanctum Concilium*, n. 10.
[106] Fr. Stefano Manelli, O.F.M., *Jesus, Our Eucharistic Love: Eucharistic Life According to the Examples of the Saints*, Manila, Philippines: Immaculata Formation House, 1973, p. 22.

The Sun of all spiritual exercises, [is] the most holy, sacred and Sovereign Sacrifice and Sacrament of the Eucharist, the very center of our Christian religion, the heart of all devotion, the soul of piety; that Ineffable Mystery which embraces the whole depth of Divine Love, by which God, giving Himself really to us, conveys all His Graces and favors to men with royal magnificence. Prayer made in union with this Divine Sacrifice has untold power.[107]

The Council of Trent taught that the best way to aid the souls in Purgatory is through the "sacrifice of the altar,"[108] that is, the Mass. This, of course, is why Catholics have for centuries had Masses said for their beloved dead. And, St. John Vianney said, "All good works taken together cannot have the value of one Holy Mass, because they are the works of men, whereas the Holy Mass is the work of God."[109]

SUNDAY MASS

Every Catholic has an obligation to attend Mass at least every Sunday. In light of all God has done for us, and the third commandment, the least we could do is spend one hour every Sunday giving thanks (as mentioned before, *Eucharist* means "thanksgiving") to Him. This is why the Church teaches:

On Sundays and other holy days of obligation the faithful are bound to participate in the Mass.... The Sunday Eucharist

---

[107] Adapted from St. Francis de Sales, *Introduction to the Devout Life*, Rivingtons, part 2, chapter 14, nn. 1, 2, p. 98, found at https://www.ccel.org/ccel/desales/devout_life/devout_life.iv.xiv.html.

[108] Council of Trent, Session 25, December 3, 1563, Decree Concerning Purgatory, found at https://www.ewtn.com/catholicism/library/twentyfifth-session-of-the-council-of-trent-1492.

[109] Fr. Stefano Manelli, O.F.M., *Jesus, Our Eucharistic Love: Eucharistic Life According to the Examples of the Saints*, p. 33.

is the foundation and confirmation of all Christian practice. For this reason the faithful are obliged to participate in the Eucharist on days of obligation, unless excused for a serious reason (for example, illness, the care of infants) or dispensed by their own pastor. Those who deliberately fail in this obligation commit a grave sin (CCC 2180, 2181; reference Code of Canon Law, nn. 1247, 1245).

Notice that shopping, playing golf or soccer or tennis, or going to a party are not mentioned as reasons to miss Sunday Mass. With the Internet and masstimes.org (a website which gives the Mass times of the ten closest churches to a given address or zip code), just about everyone should be able to find a Mass to fulfill their Sunday obligation, even when on travel.

For those who are on the edge regarding Sunday Mass, there is no question of holiness, but of fulfilling the minimum obligation of love. The person who attends Sunday Mass and says a few prayers each night is barely living the Faith, and will find it difficult to avoid losing the Faith in our secular world. Living the Faith halfway is not living the gospel; it won't satisfy the Christian heart.

A consideration that has been all but lost is that of the Lord's Day. How few Christians make any effort to avoid working on Sunday so they can worship God and rest for His sake. The *Catechism* teaches:

> On Sundays and other holy days of obligation, the faithful are to refrain from engaging in work or activities that hinder the worship owed to God, the joy proper to the Lord's Day, the performance of the works of mercy, and the appropriate relaxation of mind and body. (CCC 2185)

And, Pope John Paul II wrote, "In honouring God's 'rest,' man fully discovers himself, and thus the Lord's Day bears the profound imprint of God's blessing."[110]

One young man in our parish worked seven days a week because he felt he needed to, to support his family. At one point, he decided to step out in faith and stop working on Sundays. His income increased considerably, and he made more money in six days than he had in seven. God is ready to help us if we are willing to trust Him.

DAILY MASS

If we receive so much grace from the Mass, and we must become so very holy to be ready to enter the Kingdom, would it not be wise to consider daily Mass? St. Francis de Sales wrote:

> Strive then to your utmost to be present every day at this holy Celebration, in order that with the priest you may offer the Sacrifice of your Redeemer on behalf of yourself and the whole Church to God the Father.[111]

Whenever a person comes to me for spiritual direction, I ask them if they attend daily Mass. If not, I encourage them either to start, or, if they cannot, at least to pray that God will arrange things so that they can go. It seems that if they want help steering the ship, they should acquire the fuel themselves. In just about every case, those who have prayed for the grace of getting to daily Mass have been given it within one year.

[110] Pope John Paul II, *Dies Domini* (On Keeping the Lord's Day Holy), May 31, 1998, n. 61, found at https://www.ewtn.com/catholicism/library/jp2--dies-domini-lords-day-8153.

[111] St. Francis de Sales, *Introduction to the Devout Life*, Rivingtons, part 2, chapter 14, n. 3, pp. 98, 99, found at https://www.ccel.org/ccel/desales/devout_life/devout_life.iv.xiv.html.

I prayed for years about daily Mass before being given the grace to attend. Finally, one day, I committed to go every day for three months. If that worked out, I promised to continue for life. It did.

One friend went to one Mass during the week for a year, then two the next year, and so forth. In six years, he became a daily communicant. There are many ways to get into the grace-filled habit of daily Mass. What we should remember about this is that we should never tell God we can't go, but rather ask Him to show us how we can. It seems that this is the sort of prayer God wants to answer!

Those who know the crucial importance of remaining in the state of grace, in God's love, will make great sacrifices to get to Mass every Sunday. But, those who know the infinite value of the Mass, the superabundant grace it gives, will make great sacrifices to get to Mass every day. There is no surer way to the Kingdom.

14

EUCHARISTIC ADORATION

When I was in the seminary, I began to notice a woman who came often to pray in our chapel. I asked one of my classmates who she was. "That's Peggy," he said. "She's been making a holy hour every day for nineteen years."

"Does she have any children?" I asked.

"I think she has six."

He was right. I stopped to speak to her one day and asked how she had done it—with six children. She told me she had arranged for babysitters or arranged to trade off her children with her sisters. She would go to convents and knock on the door to use their chapel when the churches were closed, or she would come to our seminary, since our chapel was always open.

I asked her to write me a couple of pages on how she had done this so I could share her story with others when I got ordained. She agreed to do so. I had to remind her a couple of times, but finally she came up with six pages of her beautiful story.

ONE WOMAN'S NINETEEN-YEAR HOLY HOUR

She first heard about holy hours in Catholic high school, where the students all made one weekly. Even though she went to Mass daily, she was a rebel in high school; she managed to play hooky eighty-five times before the school caught her. She did everything she could to avoid doing her chores at home, and her sisters hated her for that.

When she went off to college, she began to make a holy hour each day because she was so homesick. But, once she got over being homesick, she tapered off the holy hours.

She got married at age twenty-two, and had four children in quick succession. She was still undisciplined and had no use for house work. Her husband wanted everything neat and clean. She was subject to wild mood changes, going from high to low and back again every few days. Her husband worked long hours, so she felt all alone trying to raise her four children.

When she suffered a miscarriage she became so upset that she tried to kill herself (despite her continuing to attend daily Mass and spending half an hour or more in prayer each day. Her husband was so angry with her that he refused to come to the hospital.

Because he was a morning person, and she was not, they'd have some sort of fight just about every morning. She loved her children and wanted her marriage to succeed, but she was overwhelmed. She saw no way to solve their huge personality problems.

Finally, she realized she would have to do something dramatic to turn her life around. She decided to get up each day at 4:45 a.m., an hour before her husband. Not surprisingly, it was very hard at first, but she began to see good changes almost immediately. She began to take delight in this early morning time. When she heard Bishop Sheen speak of the eucharistic holy hour, she decided that was what she needed. She made a commitment to do it every day. She would leave her children with her sister, or get a babysitter so she could make that hour.

The changes came quickly. Her moods became more even; she came to appreciate her husband, her children, and even the house she had to clean and the clothes she had to launder. By the grace of the holy hour, she learned to stay calm when her husband lost his temper instead of yelling back at him. In time, he became calmer too, and his bad temper lessened.

Her laziness was changed into vigor, her resentment into grateful acceptance. She found true peace for the first time, and came to see Jesus as her first love and constant helper. When her children were involved with drugs, she brought them in spirit to the holy hour and entrusted their lives to Jesus. She was confident He would straighten them out, and He did. One even became a daily communicant.

Peace began to reign in their home, and she and her husband learned to love each other deeply. She gave up on controlling her life and others, and just trusted all to her eucharistic love. It worked beautifully. Even in the midst of trials and sufferings, she was able to keep her peace and serenity. She found her strength each day in the Eucharist.

By God's grace, she was able to start a pregnancy aid group, and a women's prayer group. The prayer group began with just a few women; in seven years, it grew to one hundred women. About twenty of them were making a daily holy hour, and many more were making one weekly. Many of them were near divorce when they came and their families were in shambles. Through this prayer, their marriages turned around and they brought harmony to their homes.

Her closing words were as follows:

> Our Lord is a precious, wonderful, loving redeemer. He longs to touch and heal each of us in His love. He longs to give us His light and life, if only we come and let Him refresh us. I pray that you will be a holy priest, madly in love with Jesus Christ, and that you will come to know His wonderful, gentle love in the Eucharist. May you never lose sight of Him and His love.

One might ask, if the Mass is the source and summit of the Christian life, how much more could the holy hour have added to this woman's already admirable practice of daily Mass? Simply this: the deeper one's prayer life, the more perfectly a person is able to participate in the Mass, and so the more grace they are able to receive from the Mass itself. The more she prayed, the more grace she got from the Mass.

And grace she got — in abundance. What a gift she has given us in sharing that grace. Thank you, Peggy!

BISHOP SHEEN

Bishop Fulton J. Sheen is the person who seems to have popularized the eucharistic holy hour in this country. He was asked shortly before he died in 1979 what had inspired him the most. His answer was surprising. He said it was a young Chinese girl, just eleven years old.

When the Communists took power in China, they made a certain priest a prisoner in his own house. He was able to see the church from his window. One day, he saw the Communists break open the tabernacle and throw a ciborium down with all the hosts spilling out on the floor. The priest had counted the hosts, there were thirty-two.

A little girl had seen this as she prayed in the back of the church. That night, and for thirty-one more nights she came back. She snuck by the guards and prayed before the hosts for an hour to make reparation for the terrible desecration of the Eucharist. Each night, at the end of the hour, she would lean down and receive a host with her tongue, since at that time a lay person could not take the host in his hand. On the last night, when she had received the last host, one of the guards saw her leave. He followed her and beat her to death. The priest watched all this in horror.

When Fulton Sheen heard of this story, he was so moved that he resolved to spend one hour each day of his priesthood before the Blessed Sacrament. And, of course, by his talks given all over the world, he inspired many others, especially priests — myself included — to do the same. It was one of his talks on the holy hour that inspired Peggy to make her holy hour daily. And, as Bishop Sheen pointed out, it is one of the few direct requests our Blessed Lord made of His apostles: "Could you not watch one hour with Me?"[112]

It is my hope that the example of that little Chinese girl, of Bishop Sheen, and of Peggy, will inspire many reading this to do the same: spend an hour in adoration of our eucharistic Lord in the tabernacle (or exposed, if possible) each day. It is wonderful that many parishes have begun to have perpetual adoration of the Blessed Sacrament exposed in the monstrance over the past forty years. However, most of the eucharistic holy hours, including those of the saints, Bishop Sheen and Peggy as well, have been made not before the monstrance, but before the tabernacle. Although it is a great privilege to pray before the monstrance, it is almost the same thing to pray before the tabernacle. This too, is a great privilege and we should take advantage of this when exposition is not available.

Some may ask, "What would I do during an hour of prayer?" Well, here are some possibilities: meditate on Sacred Scripture, especially the readings for the next day's Mass; meditate on the Mysteries of Rosary; make the Stations of the Cross; pray the Liturgy of the Hours. Or, you might just do as a parishioner of St. John Vianney did. When asked what he did during his many hours before the Blessed Sacrament, he answered simply, "I just look at the good Lord and he looks at me."[113]

---

[112] The story of Bishop Sheen and the Chinese girl can be found at "The Little Girl Who Inspired Archbishop Sheen," from These Last Days Ministries, http://www.tldm.org/news3/sheen.htm.

[113] Adapted from Abbé Francis Trochu, *The Curé d'Ars: St. Jean-Marie Baptiste Vianney*, p. 184.

Why should you pray before the Blessed Sacrament as opposed to some other place? If the examples of Peggy and Bishop Sheen aren't enough, the saints should inspire us. St. Francis of Assisi, it seems, was the first to go and pray in churches where the Blessed Sacrament was reserved for the sick. And this custom was taken up by other saints who followed. St. Clare spent long hours in prayer before the Blessed Sacrament, and her face would glow when she came out. St. John of the Cross slept only two or three hours a night because he found his rest praying before the Blessed Sacrament. His face too, shone with brightness at times.

Pope John Paul II was said to have spent two hours a day before the Blessed Sacrament in prayer; and Mother Teresa of Calcutta and her nuns spent three hours a day there. What better way to do as our Lord has asked, "Come to me, all who labor and are heavy laden, and I will give you rest."

He will indeed refresh you.

15

SPIRITUAL READING

PRAYER ALONE WITHOUT changing us is not enough. In fact, it has been said that prayer which doesn't change us just isn't prayer. But how are we to change our lives? What are we to become? The answer lies in spiritual reading. By reading the Scriptures and the lives and writings of the saints and other holy men and women we discover what we ought to do in order to become holy. St. Jerome said, "When we pray we speak to God; but when we read [spiritual books], God speaks to us."[114] St. Francis de Sales wrote, "You should read stories in the Lives of the Saints, for there as in a mirror, you can see a picture of the Christian life and adapt their deeds to your use in keeping with your vocation."[115]

How much spiritual reading should we do each day? For most people, a good beginning would be about five pages a day. Eventually, ten pages a day would be a reasonable level to sustain a strong spiritual life. Ten pages a day may not seem like much, but that's thirty-six hundred fifty pages a year.

And, too, we should remember that spiritual reading is nothing like recreational reading. The latter is done for enjoyment whereas spiritual reading is done for formation.

[114] See Alphonsus Ligouri "On Spiritual Reading," from Our Lady's Warriors, found at http://www.ourladyswarriors.org/saints/ligoread.htm.

[115] St. Francis de Sales, *Introduction to the Devout Life*, trans. by John K. Ryan, Harper & Brothers, part 2, chapter 17, p. 108.

It's important that we not do too much spiritual reading at a time, especially if we find a particularly interesting book. We can become what we might call a "spiritual glutton," as one of my friends in the seminary did. He would find a good book on a saint and read it in just a few days. Then he would have a great let down when the next book was not so interesting. Best to read just a small amount each day for two reasons: so that "dry" reading—and some of the best spiritual books can be dry and difficult to read—will be bearable; and so that interesting reading will not move us to spend too much time reading and neglecting our prayer or work.

We should find a good time to do spiritual reading. In the seminary, nighttime reading proved best for me, just before bed. However, once I got involved in a parish, I was too tired to read at night. So, I moved reading to the morning, after morning prayers, but before I did any work for the day. Each person must discover the best time for himself and then exercise self-discipline to develop the habit of reading daily.

Scripture should always take first place in spiritual reading, but this is very rich. It should be limited to a maximum of one chapter a day. The lives of the saints, to be sure, have a special relation to Scripture. St. Francis de Sales wrote, "There is no more difference between the Gospel written and the life of a saint than between music written and music sung."[116]

There are a hundred things we must develop in order to draw close to God in love, things such as having devotion to Mary and the Sacred Heart of Jesus; loving the Church, the pope, and the teachings of the Church; delighting in the Mass and the Sacrament of the Eucharist; frequent Confession; and being willing to suffer for Christ. The only way to develop a deep and truly Catholic sense

[116] At Tony Jones, *The Sacred Way: Spiritual Practices for Everyday Life*, Grand Rapids, MI: Zondervan, 2005, p. 54.

of all these things is to read the lives and the writings of the saints. By reading a little each day, just five to ten pages, you will be stirred to a real fervor for the things of God, and you will avoid the many pitfalls in the spiritual journey. This is the most effective — and enjoyable — way to maintain growth in holiness.

By reading a biography of a saint, our defenses against changing or doing more are bypassed, since when we read about a saint they do not ask us to do more; they simply show us by example. Each time you read a book on a saint, you will undergo at least a small conversion.

There are a handful of books which have changed the lives of many readers. Here are six:

St. Francis of Assisi, by Omer Englebert
The Story of A Soul, (Autobiography of St. Thérèse of Lisieux)
Teresa of Ávila, by Marcelle Auclair
Fatima in Brief, by this author
Our Lady of Fatima, by William Thomas Walsh
Introduction to the Devout Life, by St. Francis de Sales

Notice only the last of these is a philosophical book about holiness (and, by the way, is *the* classic on the spiritual life). All the others are biographical. Whenever I give direction to someone who reads many philosophical books, I encourage them to try to get back to a biography, because these seem to be far more effective in bringing about our conversion. The things that the saints *did* are often easier to remember than the things they *wrote*.

Are anthologies of saints worthwhile? Although they can be useful, entire books about one saint will generally give you more insight into their lives and will prove more inspiring.[117]

---

[117] For some medium-length accounts of the saints, see this author's books, *Who's Who in Heaven* (Emmaus Road) and *Amazing Saints* (Catholic Faith Alive at www.cfalive.com).

St. Thérèse of Lisieux wrote, "I love to read the lives of the saints ... the account of their heroic deeds inflames my courage and spurs me on to imitate them."[118] St. Athanasius said, "You will not see anyone who is striving after his advancement who is not given to spiritual reading. And as to him who neglects it, the fact will soon be observed in his [lack of] progress."[119]

Just a few pages of reading each day will enable you to learn from the saints how to become a saint. Just about all the saints read lives of the saints. They can show us the way to the Kingdom.

---

[118] St. Thérèse of Lisieux, *St. Thérèse of Lisieux, Her Last Conversations*, p. 5.
[119] Found in Ronda De Sola Chervin, *Quotable Saints*, Ann Arbor, MI: Servant Books, 1992, p. 138.

16

LOVING NEIGHBOR:
THE SPIRITUAL WORKS OF MERCY

LOVING OUR NEIGHBOR as ourselves is the second essential law of love for the Christian. It might seem obvious to us, just what we should do to love others, but the Church actually presents us with a list of ways to love our neighbor: the spiritual and corporal works of mercy.

There are seven spiritual works of mercy:

1. instruct the ignorant;
2. counsel the doubtful;
3. admonish the sinner;
4. bear wrongs patiently;
5. forgive all injuries;
6. comfort the afflicted; and,
7. pray for the living and the dead.

INSTRUCTING THE IGNORANT

The first spiritual work of mercy is an extremely important one: instructing people about the Faith. It became fashionable in the latter part of the twentieth century for religious to give up teaching and go out to help the poor. Helping the poor is a good thing, but they were foregoing a spiritual work of mercy for a corporal. Thomas

Aquinas pointed out that the spiritual works are more beneficial than the corporal.[120]

The primary teachers of children about the Faith—and everything, for that matter—are their parents. So parents should be very concerned for their children's education, both at home and in school. St. Augustine allegedly said that the three best ways to teach children the Faith are: first, by example; second, by example; and third, by example. Every parent is a teacher simply by what he or she does and children seem to observe very well, especially when a parent makes a misstep. It is hard to overestimate the influence parents have on their children, and how important their teaching is.

Teachers in school, and especially in religion classes, should be skilled at teaching. They must avoid the two great sins of teaching, especially if they teach religion. The worst sin, of course, is to teach something other than the truth; the second is to make the subject matter boring. A religion teacher should do everything possible to make religion interesting.

One thing which keeps interest up is to teach the students about Heaven, Hell, and Purgatory in the first few classes, and then relate everything else to their salvation. There is something very interesting about one's own eternal destiny. Of course, telling stories, using the Socratic method of asking questions, and having little contests in class for those who answer the most questions correctly can help as well.

Part of instructing the ignorant is evangelizing. Christians have an obligation to spread the Faith in whatever way they can. Pope Paul VI wrote: "It is unthinkable that a person should accept the Word and give himself to the kingdom without becoming a person who bears witness to it and proclaims it in his turn."[121] Pope John

---

[120] St. Thomas Aquinas, *Summa Theologica*, II–II q32 a3, p. 1326.

[121] Pope Paul VI, *Evangelii Nuntiandi* (On Evangelization in the Modern World), December 8, 1975, n. 24, found at https://www.ewtn.com/catholicism/library/evangelization-in-the-modern-world-8990.

Paul II wrote, "Those who are incorporated in the Catholic Church ought to sense their privilege and for that very reason their greater obligation of *bearing witness to the faith and to the Christian life* as a service to their brothers and sisters and as a fitting response to God."[122] Each believer has the duty to pass on the Faith, by word, or example, or writing, or any other means available.

One woman did her part by giving out prayer cards to fellow patients while she was in the hospital. St. Maximilian Kolbe would give out Miraculous Medals to just about everyone he met. I give out a bunch of Divine Mercy holy cards to those begging at stop lights (along with a dollar) and invite them to give them out to others. One beggar told a frequent benefactor, "No need to give me money today, just holy cards. I sell them." Whatever our method, we need to spread our most precious gift: our Faith.

COUNSELING THE DOUBTFUL

The second spiritual work of mercy is to counsel those who doubt the Faith. It is similar to the first, but it is not providing information that was not already known but shoring up belief in a doctrine that was already known but was doubted. So, for example, for Harry to explain why God permits suffering in the world to help George overcome this obstacle to his faith in God, would be counseling the doubtful. Or, to explain a moral teaching to one who is doubting it would be another example.

ADMONISHING THE SINNER

Admonishing, that is, warning the sinner is another spiritual work, one which takes some skill. You must be firm enough to make the

---

[122] Pope John Paul II, *Redemptoris Missio* (On the Permanent Validity of the Church's Missionary Mandate), December 7, 1990, n. 11, found at https://www.ewtn.com/catholicism/library/missio-redemptoris-21062. In n. 72 John Paul gives examples of how the laity can evangelize.

person aware that he or she is headed for disaster, but gentle enough not to turn them off completely. For example, for Mrs. Jones to tell her twenty-five year old son six times a day that he is going to Hell because he moved in with his girlfriend will probably only result in Melvin tuning her out. But for Mrs. Jones to remind him lovingly but solemnly, at certain key times, that she is praying for his salvation might well bring about a conversion.

BEARING INJUSTICES PATIENTLY

Bearing injustices patiently also goes against our instincts as human beings. Justice is a virtue, but, bearing *injustices* for the sake of Christ is a greater virtue. This is true because such mortifications are an exercise in the virtue of loving God more than our own feelings. We think not of the world's justice, but of God's. Many a wise man has known and said: there is no justice in this world. Those who cling to their own justice in this life may well lose hold of the Kingdom of God.

Dominic Savio was once blamed for a prank that some other boys had played on their teacher. When accused, Dominic said nothing; he simply took the punishment of kneeling in the middle of the room for a long time. Before long, the other boys told the teacher that Dominic hadn't actually been the prankster. When the teacher asked Dominic why he had taken the blame, the boy replied, "Because that boy had been in trouble before and would have been expelled.... Besides, I remembered that Our Lord had once been falsely accused."[123]

FORGIVING ALL INJURIES

One of the most difficult spiritual works is forgiving all injuries. Those who spend more time contemplating their own wounds

---

[123] Found in Mary Reed Newland, *The Saints and Our Children*, New York: P. J. Kenedy and Sons, 1958, p. 52.

than the wounds of Christ will always have trouble forgiving. Perhaps that is why the saints spent such long hours meditating on Christ's sufferings. To forgive your enemy ultimately means to pray for him. Not to forgive, quite simply, is to place your feelings above his salvation.

As we mentioned earlier, forgiving is not an option. Jesus said that if we want to be forgiven by God, we must forgive others. Anyone who has found the Kingdom of God, that "pearl of great price" of which Jesus spoke, would hardly let an unforgiven injury stand in his way of possessing it, would he? If a person will not forgive, perhaps he has not yet found that "pearl" in his heart.

COMFORTING THE AFFLICTED

This work especially comes into play with the death of a loved one, but it could apply to any misfortune. Just being present for a friend who is hurting can be a great gift.

PRAYING FOR THE LIVING AND THE DEAD

Of course, in conjunction with any warning of sinners must come the spiritual work of praying for them. No real Christian could ever doubt the value of praying for another. Carlo Carretto, a devout Catholic author who spent ten years praying in the desert, wrote, "I am completely convinced that one never wastes one's time by praying; there is no more helpful way of helping those we love."[124]

Bishop Sheen once noted that the paralytic of Capernaum was healed because of the prayers and efforts of the four men who let him down through the roof. And, he had his sins forgiven as well!

---

[124] Carlo Carretto, *Letters from the Desert*, Maryknoll, N.Y.: Orbis Books, 1972; see "Letters from the Desert," from Preach the Story, found at https://preachthestory.com/letters-from-the-desert/.

A woman I knew prayed twenty-five years for her father to return to the Faith. He was reconciled to God on his deathbed. We should never lose heart in praying for those we care for.

When Mary appeared in August, 1917 to the three little seers at Fatima, she told them, "Pray, pray a great deal, and make sacrifices for sinners. Many souls go to Hell because they have no one to sacrifice and pray for them."[125] In other words, our prayers and sacrifices can actually bring people the grace to convert and be saved, when they are heading for eternal ruin.

Prayer for others is included in every Sunday Mass and in both Morning and Evening Prayer in the Liturgy of the Hours — the prayers that priests and religious are required to pray daily. St. Paul wrote, "First of all, then, I urge that supplications, prayers, intercessions, and thanksgivings be made for all men, for kings and all who are in high positions, that we may lead a quiet and peaceable life, godly and respectful in every way" (1 Tim. 2:1–2). Jesus tells us to pray for our persecutors (Matt. 5:44), and He prayed for Peter, that his faith would not fail (Luke 22:32). And Paul often asked the faithful to pray for him and promised his prayers for them.

St. Thérèse of Lisieux felt moved to pray for souls, especially great sinners, hoping to save them from being lost. She heard of a murderer named Pranzini who was about to be executed for some brutal killings. She prayed hard, offering the infinite merits of Christ, for his conversion. She also got her sister to pray for him and to have a Mass offered for him. She looked in the newspaper the day after his execution and found that although he had refused to go to Confession, when he got to the scaffold, he grabbed the

---

[125] William Thomas Walsh, *Our Lady of Fatima*, p. 120.

priest's crucifix and kissed the wounds three times. Her prayers were answered.[126]

And, how helpful it is to pray for the *dead*! In one parish the retired pastor would always "canonize" the deceased when he said a funeral Mass, thereby implicitly discouraging family and friends from praying for the deceased. All the other priests in the rectory told him not to come anywhere near their funerals. They wanted people to pray, and pray, and pray for them when they died!

St. Ambrose wrote, "Everything which we offer God out of charity for the departed is changed into merit for us, and after death we will find the hundredfold."[127] St. Gertrude offered all she could for the souls in Purgatory, and, at her death, the Lord appeared to her and told her that, for her efforts for those souls,

> I will remit ... all the [purgatorial] pains which you were to have suffered. Moreover, as I have promised a hundred-fold for those who enkindle my love, I wish to reward you further by increasing the degree of glory which awaits you above.... All the souls whom you have aided will come to lead you into [Heaven] amid great rejoicing.[128]

What is the greatest prayer we can offer for the holy souls? The Mass, as the Council of Trent taught. Both St. Jerome and St. Augustine even taught that the holy souls feel no pain during a Mass at which they are prayed for.[129]

---

[126] St. Thérèse of Lisieux, *Story of A Soul: The Autobiography of St. Thérèse of Lisieux*, trans. by John Clarke, O.C.D., Washington, DC: ICS Publications, 1975, pp. 99, 100.

[127] Bl. James Alberione, *Lest We Forget*, pp. 106, 107.

[128] Ibid., pp. 111, 112.

[129] Ibid., p. 125.

INDULGENCES

Another powerful thing we can do for the holy souls is to offer an indulgence for them. A plenary indulgence eliminates all temporal punishment due to sin. In other words it removes the need for Purgatory. A partial indulgence eliminates some of the temporal punishment. We may apply an indulgence to ourselves or to a soul in Purgatory, but not to another living person.

To gain a plenary indulgence, a number of conditions must be met:[130]

1. We must perform the indulgenced act, such as praying the Rosary in a public oratory, or in a family, religious community or other group; reading or hearing Sacred Scripture or adoring the Blessed Sacrament for at least half an hour; or, piously praying the Way of the Cross.[131]

2. A sacramental Confession, within twenty[132] days before or after the day the indulgence is sought. Thus, one Confession could satisfy for a good number of plenary indulgences.

[130] See Apostolic Penitentiary, *Manual of Indulgences*, Washington, DC: USCCB, 2006, pp. 18, 41.

[131] There are others associated with churches or certain days. For a list of works for plenary and partial indulgences, see Sacred Apostolic Penitentiary, "The Enchiridion of Indulgences," from Catholic Online, found at http://www.catholic.org/clife/prayers/indulgw.php.

[132] The traditional period of eight days was expanded to twenty days in the decree of the Apostolic Penitentiary in the Jubilee year 2000, *The Gift of Indulgence*, January 29, 2000, n. 5, found at https://www.ewtn.com/catholicism/library/gift-of-indulgence-1965. In February of 2005 the Apostolic Penitentiary confirmed, in response to a question raised by EWTN, that this norm remains in effect, and was not limited to the jubilee year: "Norm of Confession for Gaining a Plenary Indulgence," from EWTN, found at https://www.ewtn.com/catholicism/library/norm-of-confession-for-gaining-a-plenary-indulgence-1962.

3. Eucharistic Communion on the same day.

4. Prayers for the Holy Father. One Our Father and one Hail Mary suffices, but other prayers may be used.

5. Detachment from all sin, including venial sin. This does not mean freedom from all sin but rather freedom from attachment to sin. This means, in effect, that the person has no affection for sin and is sincerely trying to stop committing it.

As an example of attachment to sin, let's say someone habitually drives a little too fast, or drives too aggressively. If the person is sincerely trying to overcome this, then he is detached. If, however, the person has no intention of reforming, then he would not be a candidate for a plenary indulgence. From this it should be clear that the person seeking a plenary indulgence should be trying for the perfection of which Jesus spoke, "You, therefore, must be perfect, as your heavenly Father is perfect" (Matt. 5:48).

If a plenary indulgence is not obtained because of some attachment to a venial sin, the indulgence would still be partial. You may ordinarily receive one plenary indulgence per day, but any number of partial indulgences.

It should be noted that if all the conditions are met for a plenary indulgence, the indulgence does indeed wipe out all *our* temporal punishment due to sin if offered for ourselves, but it does not necessarily do so for a departed soul. For the dead, indulgences are offered by *suffrage*, that is, as a prayer, without certainty that it is plenary. The effects of such an indulgence are "according to the hidden designs of God's mercy."[133] Nonetheless, such an indulgence would be a powerful aid to a person in Purgatory.

[133] Bl. James Alberione, *Lest We Forget*, p. 151.

Happy the person who receives Communion at Mass daily and prays the Rosary before or after and daily fulfills all the conditions for a plenary indulgence for the holy souls in Purgatory; or, the person who offers many partial indulgences daily for the holy souls. What an army of people he will have praying for him and to greet him when he enters Heaven!

With all their power, indulgences are not as beneficial as the Mass: "In accordance with tradition, participation in the Sacrifice of the Mass or the Sacraments is not enriched by indulgences by reason of the surpassing efficacy for 'sanctification and purification' that they have in themselves."[134]

When a sister in St. Mary Magdalene de Pazzi's convent died, she and all the other sisters offered all the indulgences they had received that day for her soul. That same day she actually observed the recently deceased sister's soul ascend to Heaven as she prayed for her; Jesus appeared to St. Mary to tell her that it was due to the indulgences that this sister had so quickly been freed from the pains of Purgatory.[135]

How important it is that we never forget to pray for the dead!

[134] Apostolic Penitentiary, *Manual of Indulgences*, p. 7.
[135] Bl. James Alberione, *Lest We Forget*, p. 164.

17

LOVING NEIGHBOR:
THE CORPORAL WORKS OF MERCY

THE CORPORAL WORKS of mercy are these:

1.   feed the hungry;
2.   give drink to the thirsty;
3.   clothe the naked;
4.   shelter the homeless;
5.   visit the sick;
6.   visit the imprisoned; and,
7.   bury the dead.

Most of these come from Matthew 25:31–46 ("I was hungry and you gave me food..."), although burying the dead comes from Tobit 12.

CARING FOR THE POOR (THE FIRST FOUR CORPORAL WORKS OF MERCY)

I visited a young couple for dinner several years ago. They told me how both of them had escaped from a sinful life—working in rock bands—to find the Lord. They had given their lives over to Him entirely. They resolved when they got married that they would give 10 percent of everything to the Lord, but they were debating at one point whether they should give 10 percent of their net income after taxes, or 10 percent of their gross income. So, they asked their priest. He must have been Irish, because he answered their question with a question: "Do you want your blessings to be net, or gross?" They chose 10 percent of their gross income.

As I was having dinner with this lovely couple and their three children in a cramped apartment, it occurred to me that something was amiss. I thought: "If they have been so generous with the Lord, you would think He would provide them with better living quarters." Then the wife told me they had just bought a wonderful house at a great price in a very nice neighborhood, with a marvelous deal on the finances. They were about to move in. That completed the picture. I thought, God is always far more generous with us than we are with Him. He promised one hundredfold. What bank could give you that return — ten thousand percent — on your investment?

The first four corporal works of mercy can be combined into one: helping the poor. Each one of us has an *obligation* to help the poor, as Jesus taught in the parable of the sheep and goats. In fact, He said that when we help them we help *Him*! (Matt. 25:31–46).

The First Letter of John added to this, "But if anyone has the world's goods and sees his brother in need, yet closes his heart against him, how does God's love abide in him? Little children, let us not love in word or speech but in deed and in truth" (1 John 3:17–18).

St. Ambrose wrote, "You are not making a gift of what is yours to the poor man, but you are giving him back what is his. You have been appropriating things that are meant to be for the common use of everyone. The earth belongs to everyone, not to the rich."[136]

So, we have an obligation to help the poor, but how much? The answer is broadly given in Scripture. In the Old Testament, it

---

[136] As found in Pope Paul VI, *Populorum Progressio* (On the Development of Peoples), March 26, 1967, n. 23, found at https://www.ewtn.com/catholicism/library/populorum-progressio-21074.

is recommended that we give one-tenth of our income back to the Lord (Deut. 14:28–29; Num. 18:23–24). Some suggest that we give 5 percent to the poor and 5 percent to support the Church.

Ten percent should be the average. Some, at least for a time, might have to struggle giving 5 percent. Others may find that they can live quite comfortably giving 20 or 25 percent. How can you be morally certain that you are giving enough? It seems you should feel you have made a sacrifice. Pope John Paul II said in 1979, "You must never be content to leave [the poor] the crumbs from the feast. You must take of your substance, and not just of your abundance, in order to help them. And, you must treat them like guests at your family table."[137]

Should we give to every charity that sends us an appeal through the mail? No, probably not. If you do you may have to write hundreds of checks a year. Better to choose a few good charities and ignore the others.

There is another group of the "poor" who are often overlooked: the children in the womb. Jesus said, "I was hungry and you gave me no food ..." (Matt. 25:42); but, as Pope John Paul II wrote, "To this list also we could add other ways of acting, in which Jesus is present in each case as the *one who has been rejected*. In this way he would identify with ... the child conceived and then rejected. 'You did not welcome me!' "[138] It is not enough to be theoretically pro-life to avoid God's wrath; we must act decisively to help protect the most rejected human being in the Western world: the child in the womb. It is not enough to vote pro-life or to contribute to pro-life

[137] Pope John Paul II, Homily at Yankee Stadium, October 2, 1979, as found in "John Paul II in His Words and Others," from National Shrine of Our Lady of Lourdes, found at http://www.emmitsburg.net/grotto/father_jack/2005/pjp2a.htm.

[138] Pope John Paul II, Letter to Families, February 22, 1994, n. 22, found at https://www.ewtn.com/catholicism/library/letter-to-families-8192.

organizations (though these are fundamental). We must give witness to our loving concern for these helpless children; we must help women in crisis pregnancies, we must be passionate in our efforts to help the world see the huge social injustice of abortion in every way we can. And, we must never rest until these children are again protected by law. No one is excused from this moral battle.

SOCIAL JUSTICE

Helping the poor involves not just our individual efforts, but our commitment as a nation to help the poor. Promoting humane working conditions, just trade agreements, and fairness for immigrants are just some of the things the Church has urged us to be concerned about. There have been many social encyclicals issued by various popes. We should be aware of the teaching therein so as to understand our obligations toward the poor in the political sphere. I have listed a few these Church documents below, with a brief description of their key points. There have been many such encyclicals, but a handful follow, with a brief mention of some key points.

1. *Rerum novarum* (Pope Leo XIII, 1891): workers are to be treated not as slaves but as persons worthy of a decent wage so that they may live lives of human dignity.

2. *Quadrigesimo anno* (Pope Pius XI, 1931): socialism and unrestrained capitalism are both flawed; the wealthy ought to share their excess wealth and work for a more just distribution of goods.

3. *Mater et magistra* (Pope John XXIII, 1961): citizens ought to receive benefits from economic growth, and workers should share in a company's profits. Rich nations must be concerned for poor nations, and help them without manipulating them.

4. *Centesimus annus* (Pope John Paul II, 1991): socialism is inherently flawed because it reduces the
person to a mere cog in the economic system. Capitalism can have beneficial elements (free markets,
"private property and the resulting responsibility
for the means of production, as well as free human
creativity in the economic sector"[139]), but it is flawed
if it does not promote integral human freedom.

It is, of course, impossible to do justice to these and other such
encyclicals in just a few words, but I hope that this will provide a
taste of the Church's global concern for the poor.

IMMIGRANTS

We should remember the words of Jesus in Matthew 25:35: "I was
a stranger and you welcomed me." It seems that the Christian way
to handle immigration is not to deport all those here illegally, but
to begin with new laws which make it easier—within reason—for
immigrants to enter,[140] laws which can and will be enforced, and
then arrange some sort of fair procedure to help immigrants who
entered illegally prior to the new law to achieve legal status. The
Church taught in 2004:

[139] Pope John Paul II, *Centesimus Annus* (On the Hundredth Anni-
versary of *Rerum Novarum*), May 1, 1991, n. 42, found at https://
www.vatican.va/content/john-paul-ii/en/encyclicals/documents/
hf_jp-ii_enc_01051991_centesimus-annus.html.

[140] The second duty is to secure one's border and enforce the law for
the sake of the common good. Sovereign nations have the right to
enforce their laws and all persons must respect the legitimate exercise
of this right: "Political authorities, for the sake of the common good
for which they are responsible, may make the exercise of the right to
immigrate subject to various juridical conditions" (CCC 2241).

Christians must in fact promote an authentic *culture of welcome* capable of accepting the truly human values of the immigrants over and above any difficulties caused by living together with persons who are different. Christians will accomplish all this by means of a truly fraternal welcome in the sense of St. Paul's admonition, "Welcome one another then, as Christ welcomed you, for the glory of God." (Rom. 15:7).[141]

VISITING THE SICK

St. Catherine of Siena often visited hospitals which in her time were dirty, disease-ridden places. She always volunteered to care for those with the most repulsive diseases. One such case was a woman with an ugly case of breast cancer. Because of her stinking disease and dirty bed, hardly anyone came to take care of her. Catherine did, much to the woman's surprise. She would wait on this woman hand and foot, and showed her nothing but kindness. Instead of being grateful to Catherine for her loving care, the woman showed her hatred, and spread harmful rumors claiming Catherine had sinned against purity. Catherine ignored it all and continued to serve the woman.

Catherine's mother became angry over the rumors and told her to stay away from the woman. Catherine listened respectfully, and then knelt at her mother's feet and reminded her of all the agony Jesus endured for us—and the hatred He received in return. She asked if her mother wanted her to let the poor woman suffer a

[141] The Pontifical Council for the Pastoral Care of Migrants and Itinerant People, Instruction *Erga Migrantes Caritas Christi* (The Love of Christ Towards Migrants), May 3, 2004, nn. 39, 40, found at https://www.ewtn.com/catholicism/library/erga-migrantes-caritas-christi-2440.

miserable death without a single friend. Her mother changed her mind and praised Catherine for her goodness.[142]

Catherine prayed and prayed for the woman, and continued to serve her. Once, when the young woman entered her room, the poor woman saw Catherine clothed with a light that shone upon her and her bed, and that relieved her suffering. After this, she recognized Catherine's goodness and repented of her bad treatment. She asked Catherine to forgive her and began to tell others of Catherine's kindness and to correct the shameful lies she had spread.[143]

Jesus made it clear in Matthew 25 that visiting the sick is something we must do if we hope to enter the Kingdom. Just about all the saints were eager to visit the sick. St. Camillus de Lellis, for example, saw Christ in every sick person. He even asked them to forgive his sins. He founded an order to serve the sick in hospitals at a time when the sick were treated like dirt. A story is told of some young sisters who had just joined Mother Teresa's Missionaries of Charity. They came back from visiting the sick in a nearby hospital saying joyfully, "We have seen Jesus; we have talked to Him." Another story from Calcutta comes from a reporter who visited Mother Teresa; he found her stooped over, washing someone who had a repulsive disease. The reporter looked down at her and said, "I wouldn't do that for a million dollars." Mother Teresa looked up and replied, "Neither would I."

There are two things I learned when serving in a hospital one semester. First, you need not say much. Whether I prayed with them, or just stayed with them quietly, or just listened, they were so

---

[142] Igino Giordani, *St. Catherine of Siena*, trans. by Thomas J. Tobin, Boston: Daughters of St. Paul, 1975, pp. 63, 64.

[143] Ibid., p. 64, and Raymond of Capua, *The Life of Catherine of Siena*, trans. by Conleth Kearns, O.P., Washington, DC: Dominican Publications, 1994, p. 153.

appreciative. The other thing was that it was better to make several shorter visits than one long one. There is a certain "creative absence" that actually makes it better to take time out to call family members or go for prayer or for some nourishment, and then return. This is what I was taught and experience seemed to bear it out.

One thing that delighted me in visiting those in nursing homes was how ready the residents were for a good laugh. We have a tendency to become saddened by the surroundings, the aroma, and the condition of those living there. But the Lord doesn't invite us there to be sad. We have the ability to bring a little joy to people in these situations, and they are often quick to respond. If we have a strong prayer life and have gone to the Lord in prayer before visiting a nursing home or hospital, we will have the power to overcome the sadness of the situation with God's joy.

VISITING THE IMPRISONED

The sixth corporal work of mercy is visiting the imprisoned. Most of us don't get many chances to do this, but if we do we should jump at the chance knowing that it is Christ we visit when we go. St. Margaret of Costello, a little blind, hunch-backed girl, used to visit the local prison with her Third Order Dominican group in Costello. This was at a time when prisoners were chained day and night to the walls. There were no bathrooms, thus bringing about a disgusting stench and a breeding ground for disease. Half the prisoners died yearly of "jail fever." Margaret and her Dominican friends would go and bring clean linens, food, and the love of Christ to these poor souls.[144]

One unjustly imprisoned man who would often curse God over his sad predicament was deeply moved when Margaret stood up

---

[144] Fr. William Bonniwell, O.P., *The Life of Blessed Margaret of Castello*, Madison, WI: IDEA, Inc., 1979, p. 83.

and prayed quietly while her partner bathed his wounds. She was lifted off the ground, and her ugliness was transformed into beauty. When Margaret returned to the ground, this previously unresponsive prisoner whispered, "Little Margaret, please pray for me." He was a changed man from that point on.[145]

How much easier it is today to visit the imprisoned!

BURYING THE DEAD

Although burying the dead could literally mean just that in some remote areas, for most of us it would entail being present to those who had lost loved ones, especially at funerals and viewings. A funeral for a loved one is such a difficult time and to see a familiar face is a great consolation for family members of the deceased. While burying the dead is a corporal work of mercy it touches on two spiritual works of mercy: comforting the afflicted and praying for the (living and the) dead.

✠ ✠ ✠

The Church gives us lists of good works to help guide us in the way of loving neighbor. We ought to reflect on these works often and make every effort to practice them often.

---

[145] Fr. William Bonniwell, O.P., *The Life of Blessed Margaret of Castello*, p. 96.

PART III

The Life of Virtue

18

THE THEOLOGICAL VIRTUES: FAITH, HOPE, AND LOVE

It is necessary that your foundation consist of more than prayer and contemplation. If you do not strive for the virtues and practice them, you will always be dwarfs. — St. Teresa of Ávila[146]

WHAT IS A VIRTUE?

Before we consider the three theological virtues let's establish what a virtue is. It's a good habit regarding some activity. Some examples of virtues include loving God or practicing kindness or justice.

Living a moral life is not primarily about keeping the Ten Commandments, that is, avoiding sin, but doing good, living virtuously. That will make you holy. St. Paul speaks about virtue, tells us why we should practice it, and explains its value in his letter to the Colossians:

Put on then, as God's chosen ones, holy and beloved, compassion, kindness, lowliness, meekness, and patience, forbearing one another and, if one has a complaint against

[146] St. Teresa of Ávila, *Interior Castle*, found in *The Collected Works of St. Teresa of Ávila*, vol. II, p. 447.

another, forgiving each other; as the Lord has forgiven you, so you also must forgive. And above all these put on love, which binds everything together in perfect harmony. (Col 3:12–14).

THE VIRTUE OF FAITH

"Now faith is the assurance of things hoped for, the conviction of things not seen." (Heb. 11:1). It is believing what you cannot see or what you cannot understand. "Understanding," said St. Augustine, "is the reward of faith. Therefore do not seek to understand in order to believe, but believe that you may understand."[147] He taught that to believe or to have faith is to "think with assent."[148]

Those who were baptized as infants were given all three of the theological virtues at that time. As we grow, we are free to act on these virtues or not. How does a person grow in faith? By asking God to increase one's faith often, as did the apostles (Luke 17:5), and by seeking God's grace through prayer, the sacraments, and participation in Mass. Regarding faith, if we should choose to act on the gift of it that we received at Baptism, we are said to "have faith." Faith should begin with believing in God. Then we believe what He tells us in Sacred Scripture. Finally, because we believe, we accept His Word as the rule of our life. We don't start by examining everything God teaches and deciding if it's true. That could take forever and is often beyond our reach.

We believe in God because it makes sense, especially from the order we find in the world. We believe in Jesus as God because, among other things, He convinced at least ten skeptics to die for

---

[147] St. Augustine, Tractate 29 on the Gospel of John, n. 6, from NewAdvent, found at https://www.newadvent.org/fathers/1701029.htm.

[148] St. Thomas Aquinas, *Summa Theologica*, II–II q2 a1, p. 1179.

the truth of His Resurrection. And we believe in all that Jesus taught because God doesn't err—or lie. God actually gives us an inspiration from the Holy Spirit to move us from unbelief to belief.

At Baptism we were given the virtue of faith (and hope and love). We are free to act on these infused virtues. If we act on the gift of faith we "have faith."

FAITH AND CHURCH TEACHING

Can a person be holy if he or she rejects some Church teachings? No. For the saints, belief in Church teaching was a given. The 1983 *Code of Canon Law* states:

> A person must believe with divine and Catholic faith all those
> things contained in the word of God, written or handed on,
> that is, in the one deposit of faith entrusted to the Church,
> and at the same time proposed as divinely revealed either by
> the solemn magisterium of the Church or by its ordinary and
> universal magisterium which is manifested by the common
> adherence of the Christian faithful under the leadership of
> the sacred magisterium; therefore all are bound to avoid any
> doctrines whatsoever contrary to them.[149]

Of course, the necessity to believe all the Church teaches is itself a truth from God given to us by Jesus when He said to His apostles, "He who hears you hears me, and he who rejects you rejects me, and he who rejects me rejects him who sent me" (Luke 10:16). The descendants of the apostles are the pope and bishops. Now this only applies to teachings that are proposed as divinely revealed, either by

---

[149] *Code of Canon Law*, n. 750; found at https://www.vatican.va/archive/ cod-iuris-canonici/eng/documents/cic_lib3-cann747-755_en.html #BOOK_III.

the solemn Magisterium, that is, a solemn definition by the pope *ex cathedra*, or by the ordinary Magisterium, that is, things that are not solemnly defined.

What about teachings which are not considered divinely revealed? May a good Catholic ignore these? No. In 1964, Vatican II taught that the faithful must always hold fast to the teachings of the pope:

> This religious submission of mind and will must be shown in a special way to the authentic magisterium of the Roman Pontiff, even when he is not speaking ex cathedra; that is, it must be shown in such a way that his supreme magisterium is acknowledged with reverence, [and] the judgments made by him are sincerely adhered to.[150]

So the faithful must conform their thinking to the authentic doctrines of the Church. Although it would be seriously sinful to not accept a moral teaching of the Church, for example, the teaching on social justice or on masturbation, it would not be a sin against faith nor would it be heresy. However, the fact that one had avoided heresy in denying such moral teachings would not be much of a consolation when standing before the Lord on Judgment Day.

What of those who have never heard about Jesus Christ or of God? Are they guilty of the sin against faith? No: if a person is in blameless ignorance of God, he will be judged according to the law written in his heart to do good and avoid evil. By following this as best he can, he can be saved.

How does a person grow in faith? By asking God to increase one's faith often as did the apostles (Luke 17:5), and by seeking God's grace through prayer, the sacraments, and participating in Mass.

---

[150] Vatican II, *Lumen Gentium*, n. 25.

St. Cardinal Newman gives an insight into the believing Christian in this hymn he wrote:

> And I hold in veneration,
> for the love of [Christ] alone,
> Holy Church as His creation,
> and Her teachings as His own.[151]

THE VIRTUE OF HOPE

At a party I attended many years ago, I found myself discussing religion and God with a man perhaps in his sixties. At one point he said, "It is presumptuous to think anyone would go to Heaven." I responded, "It would be presumptuous if Christ hadn't promised it." The man was seriously lacking in the virtue of hope.

Supernatural hope is the theological virtue by which we look forward with confidence to supernatural happiness with God. It is the striving with a restless heart and patient expectation to the future good of union with God in His Kingdom. "The virtue of hope," says Josef Pieper, "is preeminently the virtue of the *status viatoris* [condition of being a pilgrim or one on the way]."[152]

As is faith, hope is something we receive freely from God at Baptism. If we act on this gift, we are said to "have hope." Faith comes first, providing the object of our hope, and then follows love, love of the good we hope for, God. Love is the greatest virtue. "So faith, hope, love abide, these three; but the greatest of these is love" (1 Cor 13:13).

---

[151] St. John Henry Newman, in the *Liturgy of the Hours*, vol. IV, New York: Catholic Book Publishing Co., 1975, p. 628.

[152] Josef Pieper, *Faith, Hope, Love*, trans. Richard and Clara Winston and Sr. Mary F. McCarthy, S.N.D., San Francisco: Ignatius Press, 1997, p. 98.

Hope initially strives for the reward of Heaven for the self, but, as we deepen our love for God, we seek to be with God for His sake. This is because we are grateful to Him and we wish Him the happiness of possessing us in love, since that is why He created us. Nonetheless, the initial hoping for Heaven for our own sake is something good, as was taught by the Council of Trent.[153]

Our hope is based on the death and Resurrection of Jesus. It is "through Him [that] we have become certain of God."[154]

And it is in prayer that our hope is begun. Pope Benedict XVI taught, "A first essential setting for learning hope is prayer."[155]

While we should have confidence that we will end in God's Kingdom if we live in His way, we should have a healthy fear of losing it, while we still have free will. The Council of Trent warned of this:

> Let no one promise himself any security about this gift with absolute certitude, although all should place their firmest hope in God's help. For, unless they themselves are unfaithful to His grace, God, who began the good work, will bring it to completion, effecting both the will and the execution. Yet, "let anyone who thinks he stands take heed lest he fall" (1 Cor. 10:12) and let him "work out his salvation in fear and trembling" (Phil. 2:12) in labors, in vigils, in almsgiving, in prayers and offerings, in fasting and chastity. Knowing that

---

[153] J. Neuner, S.J. and J. Dupuis, S.J., *The Christian Faith in the Doctrinal Documents of the Catholic Church*, New York: Alba House, 1996, n. 1976, p. 764.

[154] Pope Benedict XVI, *Spe Salvi*, (In Hope We Are Saved), November 30, 2007, n. 26, found at https://www.ewtn.com/catholicism/library/spe-salvi-in-hope-we-are-saved-3355.

[155] Ibid., n. 32.

they are reborn unto the hope of glory and not yet unto glory, they should be in dread about the battle they still have to wage with the flesh, the world and the devil.[156]

NATURAL AND SUPERNATURAL HOPE

There is another sort of hope, natural hope, which, according to Josef Pieper, "blossoms with the strength of youth and withers when youth withers." Pieper goes on to quote the *Summa* of St. Thomas Aquinas: "For youth, the future is long and the past is short."[157] When we are children we often believe we will be professional athletes when we grow up, we'll be quite successful and rich, and, of course, we'll never grow old. As we grow older, we realize that many of the unrealistic dreams we had will not happen. This seems to be at the heart of the mid-life crisis, in which we ask, "Is that all there is?" The more we are concerned with this world rather than the next, the more unpleasant this crisis is.

Supernatural hope, on the other hand, is a constant source of youthfulness because it provides an eternal future and thus should be an excellent remedy for the mid-life crisis. Who can deny the youthfulness of St. Teresa of Ávila or St. John Bosco, even in their later years, or, closer to our own time, the youthfulness of Mother Teresa of Calcutta?

SINS AGAINST HOPE

There are two sins against hope: despair and presumption. Despair kills hope by denying there is anything to hope for. One who despairs sees his own sins as unforgivable, greater than God's mercy.

---

[156] J. Neuner, S.J. and J. Dupuis, S.J., *The Christian Faith in the Doctrinal Documents of the Catholic Church*, n. 1942, p. 757.

[157] St. Thomas Aquinas, *Summa Theologica*, I–II q40 a6, as found in Josef Pieper, *Faith, Hope, Love*, p. 110.

On the other hand, presumption kills hope by presuming salvation. One guilty of presumption convinces himself that he has somehow arrived at the state of salvation and is unable to go astray. "There are two things that kill the soul," said St. Augustine, "despair and false hope."[158] Both destroy our status as pilgrims on our way to God, a status which is necessary for us in order to practice the virtue of hope.[159]

The mercy of God is far greater than all sins put together. God the Father told St. Maria Faustina, "Encourage souls to place great trust in My fathomless mercy. Let the weak, sinful soul have no fear to approach Me, for even if it had more sins than there are grains of sand in the world, all would be drowned in the immeasurable depths of My mercy."[160]

Where does despair come from? According to St. Thomas Aquinas, it often comes from disordered sexual activity or lust, as St. Thomas Aquinas taught, but it more often comes from sloth. The love of sexual pleasures often causes a distaste for spiritual things by comparison. They are not stimulating enough compared to sexual activity. As a result, a person despairs of ever attaining spiritual wholeness again, thinking that he will never be able to detach himself from unbridled sex. What he fails to realize is that, after a time of painful withdrawal from lust, the spiritual life becomes sweet again. Sloth, on the other hand, is a sadness over the divine good in mankind, over the fact that we are created in the image and likeness of God, and that we can be great by God's grace. Rather than call on God for help, the slothful person gives up.

---

[158] St. Augustine of Hippo, *Sermons*, 87, 8, found in Josef Pieper, *Faith, Hope, Love*, p. 113.

[159] Josef Pieper, *Faith, Hope, Love*, p. 113.

[160] St. Maria Faustina, *Divine Mercy in My Soul: Diary of Saint Maria Faustina Kowalska*, n. 1059, pp. 399, 400.

The terrible thing about despair is that there is not even an ounce of pleasure in it. God the Father said this to St. Catherine of Siena: "There is no pleasure and nothing but intolerable suffering in [despair]. One who despairs despises My mercy, making his sin to be greater than mercy and goodness."[161]

Presumption is a far more prevalent sin against hope in our day. It is the belief that one is assured of salvation. We should remember the words of St. Paul quoted above: "Work out your own salvation with fear and trembling" (Phil. 2:12).

Perhaps just as harmful as presumption is one's limited, or even negative, adult image of Heaven. A healthy idea of Heaven, as I have mentioned above, is a wonderful incentive to keep struggling, to allow the Lord to transform us and make us a new creation in Christ. And. a concept that will keep us from being selfish in our hope is this very fact that we are to become a new creation for God, that we might be a pleasing gift to Him in His Kingdom. This wishing God goodness and glory is why we should strive for perfection; We want Him to possess something good when He possesses us. "They who wait for the LORD shall renew their strength, they shall mount up with wings like eagles, they shall run and not be weary, they shall walk and not faint." (Isa. 40:31)

THE VIRTUE OF CHARITY (LOVE)

Many years ago, I brought Communion to a man dying of cancer. He told me that he had left his wife some years before for a younger woman, with whom he had lived for several years. Then, when he got cancer, the woman wanted nothing more to do with him. He asked his wife if she would take him back, and she did. She took care of him until he died. That was a classic example of the virtue of charity.

---

[161] St. Catherine of Siena, *The Dialogue of St. Catherine of Siena*, p. 267.

The *Catechism* teaches, "Charity is the theological virtue by which we love God above all things for his own sake, and our neighbor as ourselves for the love of God" (CCC 1822). This, of course, comes from the two great commandments of love that Jesus taught when asked what was necessary to attain eternal life: "You shall love the Lord your God with all your heart, and with all your soul, and with all your strength, and with all your mind; and your neighbor as yourself" (Luke 10:27). The word here in the original Greek text is the verb *agapao*, which is derived from *agape*.

It seems that the meaning of this love is a giving of self for the good of the beloved without conditions. This is the way God loves us, and it is this love we must learn and make a habit in order to be ready to live in the Kingdom. It is not an indiscriminate self-giving but a benevolent one. To put it more simply, this love is to make other peoples' lives better regardless of their merits.

LOVING OUR ENEMIES

Jesus showed us a new kind of love when He prayed for those who crucified Him. He empowers us to love friend *and* enemy:

> You have heard that it was said, "You shall love your neighbor and hate your enemy." But I say to you, Love your enemies and pray for those who persecute you, so that you may be sons of your Father who is in heaven; for he makes his sun rise on the evil and on the good, and sends rain on the just and on the unjust. For if you love those who love you, what reward have you? Do not even the tax collectors do the same? And if you salute only your brethren, what more are you doing than others? Do not even the Gentiles do the same? You, therefore, must be perfect, as your heavenly Father is perfect. (Matt. 5:43–48)

What an amazing development, this love of enemies. Jesus has taught us how to love as God loves, and this loving of enemies is, it seems, the key to perfection.

What is self-love? Not, as some have suggested, self-esteem, but rather a concern for our own good. C. S. Lewis calls this "need love." This would include things like getting adequate sleep, nutrition, and recreation, as well as pursuing our spiritual needs, which are primary. Taking adequate care of ourselves (without pampering ourselves) is part of the virtue of humility. While it is true that the saints denied themselves all sorts of things to make reparation for sins, some had to cut back their penances because they exceeded prudence and made themselves sick. Prudence, as we will see, is not an option for the Christian.

The *Catechism* statement above that we must love our neighbor for God's sake, gives real power to our love. It means we can love others truly unconditionally since we are not dependent on a human reward as a motive. When we love others for God's sake, God assures us a reward. Thus we can persevere indefinitely in the love of a troublesome spouse or others since we are both empowered and rewarded by God.

This, no doubt is what moved St. Monica to love her philandering husband for so many years, before her charity and kindness converted him; and what empowered Bl. Anna-Maria Taigi to love her rough, angry husband. Both chose to seek their fulfillment not from their spouses, but from God. And God ended up giving them fulfillment from both.

FINAL THOUGHTS ON LOVE

Love can never be separated from the cross. Mother Teresa of Calcutta said, "Love, to be true, has to hurt."[162] Bishop Sheen would ask

---

[162] "Mother Teresa," from Ascension Research Center, found at http://www.ascension-research.org/teresa.html.

rhetorically if we had any scars from our loving. To love someone often means to surrender our will to their good and that is where the cross begins.

We should never stop trying to grow in love, fearless of the hurt. God revealed to St. Catherine of Siena how He works in the soul to attain this end: "The soul is never so perfect in this life that she cannot attain to a higher perfection of love."[163]

"So faith, hope, love abide, these three; but the greatest of these is love" (1 Cor. 13:13).

---

[163] St. Catherine of Siena, *The Dialogue of St. Catherine of Siena*, p. 196.

19

THE CARDINAL VIRTUES:
PRUDENCE, JUSTICE, FORTITUDE, AND TEMPERANCE

Prudence is the first of the four cardinal, or "hinge," virtues, the others being justice, fortitude, and temperance. These are the four main virtues of the moral life, upon which all the other virtues depend — or hinge.

Prudence is what inspires me to repay the hundred dollars I borrowed from Melvin last week; justice is what compels me to pay it. Prudence is what inspires us to decide it's time to get to bed; fortitude compels us to do it when we'd rather stay up and watch a ball game. And, prudence is what tells us that two servings of Thanksgiving turkey are enough; temperance compels us to stop eating.

PRUDENCE: ACTING REASONABLY

A couple once went to see a priest and indicated they wanted to marry. They had known each other for just six months, and were both only in their late teens. The priest asked if they knew how slim their chances of success were. They admitted that they might be one in twenty. However, they assured the priest that they were the one in twenty who *would* succeed. He asked them if perhaps all those who had failed had believed *they* really were the one in twenty. They conceded that point as well, but said they really *were* the one in twenty. The priest urged them to take some time to reconsider, and they agreed under duress. But it was clear that they had no intention of changing their plans. This is a classic example of what prudence is *not*. (They never did marry.)

Prudence, according to the *Catechism*, is "the virtue that disposes practical reason to discern our true good in every circumstance and to choose the right means of achieving it.... Prudence is 'right reason in action,' writes St. Thomas Aquinas, following Aristotle" (CCC 1806). It is the virtue that guides us to act reasonably.

Prudence requires us to think before acting. Legalism is a way to avoid thinking, by sticking to laws whether they apply or not. Situation ethics is the opposite extreme, whereby we think too much, denying moral absolutes and deciding right and wrong based on our own subjective opinions.

Prudence is also what enables us to see that we need not accept evil mixed with the good in our recreation. For example, we need not partake of entertainment which includes bad language, sex, or other evils. Some, especially the young, argue, "Well, there is a lot of good material in some of these movies!" In response, the analogy made is that of the person who made brownies with the best of ingredients, but added only one tablespoon of dog excrement. Would you eat it? To the best of my knowledge, no one has yet volunteered to try such brownies. So, it seems, we are more careful about what enters our stomachs than what enters our souls.

There are many analogous recreational activities, such as watching tainted television shows, attending parties that involve drugs, excessive drinking, or other harmful things; smoking; or reading books with some objectionable passages. Those who are truly striving for holiness know that there are enough good forms of recreation that we need not compromise with the evils of the world. With a little creativity, we can find wholesome activities, such as sports, religious social activities, good movies, and books. Not everything that is fun is "sinful or fattening."

Of course, even good recreation can be overdone. If we are playing golf or tennis at every opportunity, regardless of our obligations, we are not being prudent (or temperate). We are being selfish.

JUSTICE: GIVING WHAT IS DUE

Some time ago, a woman bought something in a grocery store. When she returned home, she discovered she had been undercharged. So, the next time she went to that store, she pointed out the error to the store manager and paid him the twenty dollars she owed. He was so surprised and delighted that he invited her to take a couple of pies as his gift to her for her honesty. She acted in justice.

As a boy, I took music lessons and paid for all but the last lesson. I fell into the worldly attitude, "If I can get away with it, I'll forget about it." However, the teacher was my friend's father, and every time I saw him, he reminded me of the debt. I'm sure he didn't need the money, but he wanted me to learn justice. In the end, I got the money and paid him. I learned more from his insistence on justice than I did from the music lessons.

> *Justice* is the moral virtue that consists in the constant and firm will to give their due to God and neighbor. Justice toward God is called the "virtue of religion." Justice toward men disposes one to respect the rights of each and to establish in human relationships the harmony that promotes equity with regard to persons and to the common good. (CCC 1807)

Put simply, justice involves giving what is due.

How important is justice? It is very important. Sacred Scripture refers more than eight hundred times to "justice" and the "just man," the latter meaning "the good, the holy man." Cicero declared "Good men are called so chiefly from their justice."[164]

A classic question of justice has to do with unauthorized copying of music, or movies, or computer programs. Do not those who created these things have a right to some recompense? It is unjust to share these things with others without permission. This may come as a shock to some, but it shows how easily we can let justice slide.

There are several parts of justice. We will consider: piety, obedience, gratitude, and truthfulness.

PIETY

Piety is showing the honor and veneration due to God, parents, and country — in other words, to anyone who provides for our well-being and governance. The veneration due to God is called *religion*. St. Augustine taught that the word *religion* came from the Latin *religare*, meaning to bind up. So, in religion, we bind ourselves to God in worship, adoration, and reverence. Since God has created us and given us everything we have, we *owe* Him our prayer, our worship, our participation in the Mass, and our contributions to the Church and to the poor.

Part of religious piety is to dress up for Mass. Does Sacred Scripture say anything about this? It does indeed! "Worship the LORD in holy array" (1 Chron. 16:29; Ps. 29:2; 96:9). What does the Church say? "Bodily demeanor (gestures, clothing) ought to convey the respect, solemnity, and joy of this moment when Christ becomes our guest [in holy Communion]" (CCC 1387). Devotees of Pope John Paul II's theology of the body should have no problem with this since one of his main points was that the body expresses the person.

---

[164] Josef Pieper, *The Four Cardinal Virtues*, Notre Dame, IN: Notre Dame Press, 1966, p. 64.

Genuflection should be included under piety as well: "At the name of Jesus, every knee should bend, of those in heaven, on earth and beneath the earth" (Phil. 2:10).[165] Undoubtedly, it is from this passage that our long tradition of genuflecting before the Eucharist in the tabernacle or monstrance is based.[166] A half genuflection seems to be such a (public) irreverence that those who cannot genuflect might do better to simply bow profoundly as is the Eastern Rite (Catholic) custom.

Another aspect of piety is to make a sign of reverence before receiving Holy Communion. In the United States, our bishops have asked that we bow before stepping up to receive.

Piety toward human beings involves honoring parents and country. Patriotism is a part of the virtue of piety, that is, a part of justice.

OBEDIENCE

Obedience is another part of justice, and it is one of the most important virtues for the spiritual life. St. Gregory the Great said, "Obedience should be practiced not out of servile fear, but from a sense of love, not through fear of punishment, but through love of justice."[167] So, obedience should stem from love, as should all the virtues, including justice itself—since love, or charity, "is the *form of [all] the virtues*" (CCC 1827).

We will have more on obedience in a later chapter.

[165] Author's translation.

[166] Sacred Congregation for Divine Worship, *Eucharistiae Sacramentum* (The Sacrament of the Eucharist), June 21, 1973, n. 84, found at https://www.ewtn.com/catholicism/library/eucharistiae-sacramentum-2209: "Genuflection in the presence of the blessed sacrament, whether reserved in the tabernacle or exposed for public adoration, is on one knee."

[167] Found in St. Thomas Aquinas, *Summa Theologica*, II–II q104 a3, p. 1643.

GRATITUDE

In our affluent Western world, we often forget to be grateful. And we certainly have a lot to be grateful for. For example, we may say grace before meals, but do we say grace after meals? "We give you thanks Almighty God, for all the benefits received from your bounty, and may the souls of the faithful departed through the mercy of God rest in peace. Amen." There are those who are constantly grateful for every little thing in their life, and there are those who are constantly complaining. Which do you think are the happiest?

In fact, there have been clinical studies that show that people who express their gratitude for three or four things each day are much less likely to get depressed. Thankfulness is good for your mental *and* your spiritual health!

TRUTHFULNESS

Another part of justice is truthfulness. When we speak, we are obliged in justice to speak the truth. Does that mean we are always obliged to tell all the truth we know? Not at all. We may withhold the truth if the person to whom we are speaking has no right to it.

To withhold the truth, we may either refuse to answer, or evade the question, or say something which is true in one sense but not in another. St. Thomas Aquinas wrote, "Therefore it is not lawful to tell a lie in order to deliver another from any danger whatever. Nevertheless it is lawful to hide the truth prudently, by keeping it back, as Augustine says."[168] For example, if a woman walks in with the ugliest hat in all the world and asks her employee how he likes her new hat, he might reply, "It's out of this world." Of course, if a parent asks a child about his homework or how he did on an

[168] St. Thomas Aquinas, *Summa Theologica*, II–II q110 a3 reply obj. 4, p. 1666.

exam, the child must answer truthfully, since a parent has a right to that information.

So, in summary, justice involves giving what is due, and it includes piety, obedience, gratitude, and truthfulness.

FORTITUDE (DIFFICULT YESES OR NOS)

When St. Thomas More refused to sign documents declaring King Henry VIII head of the Catholic Church in England, and the legitimacy of his (illegitimate) children by Ann Boleyn, he was found guilty of treason. After suffering for fifteen months as a prisoner in the Tower of London, More was beheaded on July 6, 1535. He was beatified in 1886 and canonized in 1935. His willingness to die for his Faith and the truth is considered a classic example of fortitude.

What is the virtue of fortitude? It is the virtue which empowers a person to overcome great difficulties to do what is good. Josef Pieper wrote:

> Fortitude presupposes vulnerability; without vulnerability there is no possibility of fortitude. An angel cannot be brave, because he is not vulnerable. To be brave actually means to be able to suffer injury. Because man is by nature vulnerable, he can be brave.[169]

So, in order to practice the virtue of fortitude, we must be able to be injured, and the worst bodily injury is death. So according to St. Thomas Aquinas, fortitude is ultimately concerned with the danger of death in a battle [to do good].[170] If, for example, the evil emperor knew that a certain Christian would endure anything for his Faith but death, he need only threaten the Christian with death, and he would give up the Faith.

---

[169] Josef Pieper, *The Four Cardinal Virtues*, p. 117.
[170] See ibid.

How is it possible to bear martyrdom? It seems impossible without God's grace. When St. Felicity gave birth to a baby while she was in prison, awaiting execution for being a Christian, she cried out in great pain while in labor. The others asked how she would endure her cruel martyrdom if this bothered her so much. Her reply was, "Today, it is I who suffer in giving birth, but then Another will suffer in me, because I shall suffer for Him."[171]

In our everyday living, we need the virtue of fortitude to function, sometimes just to get out of bed in the morning. Another critical area where fortitude is needed is that of communication, especially about displeasure over another's bad behavior. We risk their angry response, or even losing their friendship. However, if we do not communicate our displeasure, our relationship with the other person may gradually disintegrate.

Fortitude is extremely important for the spiritual life for two reasons. First, purgation from our sins and vices is a painful process which we must go through to get closer to God. And, second, we must endure the dryness of finding no consolation in prayer, when God withdraws and invites us to let go of all His gifts and cling to Him alone.

TEMPERANCE (DIFFICULT NOS)

What do workaholics, "computerholics," sex addicts, alcoholics, television addicts, overeaters, addictive gamblers, and love addicts have in common? They are all missing the virtue of temperance.

Temperance is the habit of moderating the attracting appetites in accord with reason. Now the attracting appetites are many. They consist primarily of those involving food, drink, and sex. These are

---

[171] Found in Enzo Lodi, *Saints of the Roman Calendar*, trans. by Jordan Aumann, O.P., New York: Alba House, 1992, p. 67.

generally considered the most powerful appetites, and it is no accident that these strongest appetites are most closely associated with human flourishing. Eating and drinking ensure individual survival. Sex ensures survival of the entire human race.

When our appetites are not ordered properly, that is, when they are not governed by right reason, they become like spoiled brats. They want their own way; they do not know when to stop; the more they get, the more they want. And, like a child, disordered appetites can be corrected by being restrained. But restraining children is not enough, and neither is it enough to simply restrain the appetites. If you restrain children without ever training them to behave, they will merely wait for a time when you are not there, and then explode in a binge of self-gratification. In other words, children must be taught to see the good reasons for their restraints so they can make those restraints their own.

So it is with the appetites. St. Thomas Aquinas taught that the appetites listen not only to reason, but also to imagination and the senses. So it is not enough to simply exert self-control over the appetites like some dictator. If you do, they will wait for a moment of weakness and then explode. We see this when a young man, for example, curbs his sexual appetite by simply saying "No, no, no," over and over again, thereby repressing it. After doing well for six weeks or so, all of a sudden he goes wild. That's called "white knuckle chastity."

The appetites, say Aristotle and St. Thomas, must be treated politically, that is, they must be persuaded. Pope John Paul II wrote,

> [The will is] constantly confronted by a value which fully explains the necessity for containing impulses aroused by carnal desire and sensuality. Only as this value takes

possession of the mind and will does the will become calm and free itself from a characteristic sense of loss.[172]

That is, the appetites, whether sexual or other, must be convinced by reason so that they appear to participate in the reasoning process themselves. In this way, they become trained to act habitually in accord with right reason. Only then can a person claim to have the virtue of temperance.

In the case of the young man, rather than just saying no, he should have said, "No, *and* here's why." Eventually, through perseverance, the inordinate appetites just give up and admit, "Okay, okay, you're right. I give in. That won't make me happy."

Success at saying no to the appetites when appropriate is continence, or self-control, whereas training the appetites not to get stirred up at all when inappropriate is temperance. Self-control, then, involves a struggle whereas temperance forgoes an attractive but immoral object with serenity.

Now, there are several parts of temperance: chastity, abstinence, sobriety, and purity.

CHASTITY

As an example of how to "convert" the sexual appetite, a young man struggling with chastity some years ago began at my request to read the following list of reasons why he should be chaste:

1. Sex is holy, not a plaything. It should never be trivialized.
2. Created in the image of God, I can live by reason, not just by urges (as the animals do).
3. Persons are to be loved, not merely used as objects of enjoyment.

---

[172] Karol Wojtyła, *Love and Responsibility*, trans. by H. T. Willetts, New York: Farrar, Straus, Giroux, 1981, p. 198.

4. I must not treat persons as objects, even in the mind, lest I become a user of persons in practice.

5. Unchaste activity destroys my most precious friendship, that with God, the source of all happiness.

6. Unchaste activity brings pleasure but not happiness.

After reading this list several times a day for a year, he told me he had found peace. He had no more struggles to be chaste. Another young man who had struggled with pornography addiction for twenty years was able to just about eliminate pornography after reading the card daily for a couple of years. This method—giving yourself the reasons to avoid harmful things—can be applied to any of the appetites: for food, for drink, for a dysfunctional love, for gambling, and so forth. Ultimately, we are more attracted to the truth than to pleasure.

The *norm* for chastity is as follows: "Sexual pleasure is morally disordered when sought for itself, isolated from its procreative and unitive purposes."[173] The unitive purpose implies the celebration of the existing marital love covenant of the couple. Sexual pleasure may be sought only in marriage. And, the "procreative purposes" means the act itself is open to having children, regardless of the intention of the (married) couple. In other words it must be a complete marital act. It is not licit to seek sexual pleasure apart from a complete, uncontracepted marital act.[174]

ABSTINENCE

Abstinence is the virtue of refraining from food or drink in accord with right reason. So, the diabetic who avoids sweets consistently has the virtue of abstinence. So does the person who is allergic to milk and stays away from milk products. So does the person who

---

[173] CCC 2351.

[174] For a more detailed treatment of chastity, see my book *Acheiving Chastity in a Pornographic World* at www.cfalive.com.

never over-indulges in food or drink. (It seems this is not a terribly popular virtue in our Western world.)

Under the virtue of abstinence comes fasting. Fasting, according to St. Thomas Aquinas, has three purposes. The first is to control the disordered desires of the flesh, not just the desire for food and drink but all the desires of the flesh, including sexual desires. St. Jerome explained that "Venus is cold when Ceres and Bacchus are not there."[175] In other words, lust is diminished by giving up food and drink.

The second reason for fasting is to free us to reflect on our eternal goal. If we are thinking about food all the time, it is hard to keep our attention on the spiritual life. The third reason for fasting is to make reparation for sin, one's own sins and the sins of the world. St. Augustine summed up the value of fasting, saying that it "cleanses the soul, raises the mind, subjects one's flesh to the spirit, renders the heart contrite and humble, scatters the clouds of concupiscence, quenches the fire of lust, and kindles the true light of chastity."[176]

Fasting is not an option for the Christian. Jesus told the Pharisees his disciples would fast once he had left them: "The days will come, when the bridegroom is taken away from them, and then they will fast in that day" (Mark 2:18–20). St. Thomas Aquinas wrote, "Fasting is useful as atoning for and preventing sin, and as raising the mind to spiritual things; and everyone is bound by the natural dictate of reason to practice fasting as far as it is necessary for these purposes."[177]

---

[175] Found in St. Thomas Aquinas, *Summa Theologica*, II–II q147 a1, p. 1785.

[176] Ibid.

[177] *Summa Theologica*, II–II q147 a6, p. 1393.

And, according to Canon Law, all Christians are obliged to fast. "The divine law binds all the Christian faithful to do penance each in his or her own way."[178]

Fasting applies not only to food, but to other enjoyable things such as listening to music or watching television. Fasting or doing penance is primarily about denying the will, not just the body. The Lord told St. Catherine of Siena, "Whoever wants for my sake to mortify his body with many penances and not his own will does not please me much."[179] And, of course, fasting or doing penance must always be done with prudence. Fasting to the point of ruining your health is not pleasing to God, as St. Bernard learned the hard way.

Moderation in the use of television is of great importance in this age, especially for the young. One young mother got rid of the family television as an experiment. Within two weeks she saw a great improvement in the behavior of her children. The television never returned. Television seems to have an addictive power over some people. Unfortunately, it often has little to offer. When I got ordained, I resolved never to watch television except on Sundays and feast days. What a blessing that has been! Because of television's addictive power, I do recommend designating most days as television-free days.

Sobriety is another part of temperance. No one can be holy if they overindulge in drink. A similar approach to that regarding chastity may be applied to sobriety.

DETACHMENT

Detachment is an extremely important element of holiness and is part of temperance. To be detached, in a spiritual context, is to enjoy things

---

[178] *Code of Canon Law*, n. 1249; found at https://www.vatican.va/archive/cod-iuris-canonici/eng/documents/cic_lib4-cann1244-1253_en.html#TITLE_II.

[179] St. Catherine of Siena, *The Dialogue of St. Catherine of Siena*, p. 55.

without being dependent on them. An attachment is something or someone we feel we *must* have in order to be happy, whether it be a computer game, a car, certain foods—or a boyfriend or girlfriend. What the Christian needs to be happy is God and whatever He gives us for the moment. Every attachment is in competition with God. Everything in second place is a threat to what is in first.

One of Satan's ploys is to get us to attach to the pleasures of this world, to make us forget about the next. To be worldly means to be so concerned about this world that we have little time for God, for loving Him and neighbors. Even success can be a dangerous thing if it distracts us from God or becomes our primary goal. Our citizenship is in Heaven (Phil. 3:20), not here, where we are just travelers.

Being attached to God above all is a beautiful way to live. In this way we possess our things; they don't possess us. We are not always worried about losing what we have, but are happy we have them for now. If we lose them, we stay focused on the Lord and try to forget about them. Our attitude should be that of Job who said, "Naked I came from my mother's womb, and naked shall I return; the LORD gave, and the LORD has taken away; blessed be the name of the LORD" (Job 1:21).

It sounds cold to be "detached" from a friend or a girlfriend, or even a spouse, but that is a different kind of detachment. To be detached spiritually means to love others primarily for their sake and especially for God's sake, and not for our own sake. It means we love people, not for the pleasure they give us, but for their good and to please God. Granted, we get pleasure from loving people, and we should enjoy that pleasure, but we should never cling to it, making it a priority. To make pleasure the most important thing in any endeavor is to be a hedonist.

Alas, many of us have been hedonists from time to time, but hedonism is not a part of holiness. We should constantly remind ourselves that happiness comes from love, not pleasure.

PARTS OF TEMPERANCE

Now there are several virtues which are associated with temperance, or are means of attaining it. We will consider three: continence (i.e., self-control), humility, and modesty.

Continence, as we mentioned earlier, is that self-control one needs to keep from falling for an unreasonable desire while developing the virtue of temperance, but before acquiring it. One exercises continence by looking at the pecan pie covered with ice cream and thinking, "Oh, I would love to eat that, but I really shouldn't. The doctor told me to lose twenty pounds, but it looks *so* good. No, no, no! I *am* going to lose weight; and I'm going to start right now." That's continence. You have a struggle, and you win. With temperance, you look at that same piece of pie and think, "Nice, but not for me. I've said no the last fifty times, and I'll say no this time too. My diet is working, and I feel good about it. No problem!"

Humility is part of temperance, too, since it involves moderating the appetite for praise. We need the affirmation of praise from time to time, just as we need food. We should be detached from both. Humility helps us to be *detached* from praise, not depending on it for our happiness. If we love, we will get praise, and that's fine, but if we don't get praise, we still love, because it's loving that makes us happy. When the humble person is praised, he need not deny he has done something good, but he will give most of the credit to God.

Humility of course is an elusive virtue, because you struggle to attain it, and finally you say to yourself, "Ah, at last I am humble!"—you've lost it! The person who is truly humble is deeply aware of his tendency to be proud. This is the paradox of humility. A young woman confessed to Bishop Sheen once and started out by saying, "I am the worst girl in the city of New York." He replied, "You are not the worst girl in the city of New York. The worst girl in the city of New York says that she is the best girl in the city of New York."[180]

Modesty is also a part of temperance, but it pertains to less attractive goods. The desire we most often associate with immodesty is that of being noticed, or highly regarded. It is certainly not wrong to look nice, but that should not be overdone, to the point where we take a long time to "primp." St. Francis de Sales wrote, "For my part, I would have devout people, whether men or women, always be the best dressed in a group but the least pompous and affected. As the proverb says, I would have them 'adorned with grace, decency and dignity.'"[181] Modesty of dress bears a special relationship to chastity, which is all but forgotten in our age. Women have much to lose by dressing immodestly and should be alerted to this from a young age. Alas, there are many good women who have barely a clue as to how men are interiorly responding to the way they dress.[182]

Of course, using computers, especially the Internet, is another good which should be moderated by temperance. I use alarm software to regulate my use of the computer, with alarms going off at prayer times, dinner times, bedtime, and the like. The use of cellular phones needs to be tempered as well, especially among teenagers.

The trouble with these seemingly harmless addictions to television, computers, and phones is that they develop a mindset, especially among the young, of seeking pleasure without reference to reason. Those who run free with the use of television or computers

---

[180] Ven. Fulton Sheen, *Treasure in Clay: The Autobiography of Fulton J. Sheen*, Garden City, NY: Doubleday, 1980, p. 268.

[181] St. Francis de Sales, *Introduction to the Devout Life*, Image Books, part 3, chapter 25, p. 193.

[182] See author's article on modesty at https://cfalive.com/products/a-modesty-proposal.

when they are young are good candidates for addiction to alcohol, drugs, and sex when they are older.

Workaholism is another area of addiction which needs to be moderated by temperance. Some feel so fulfilled by their work that they neglect family, health, or even a normal social life. Again, reason must govern the Christian.

So, temperance is an important virtue that involves difficult nos to pleasant things. But a no to pleasure can be a yes to reason and happiness. The dignity of a human person includes the ability to live by reason, in the image of God. If we hope to live with Him in the Kingdom, we need to have this virtue—and all the others as well.

20

LIVING SIMPLY: THE OBLIGATION OF EVERY CHRISTIAN

EVERY CHRISTIAN IS called to live simply. Fr. Thomas Dubay wrote in *Happy Are You Poor*, "Scripture scholars seem to be of one mind . . . that most New Testament texts that deal with poverty as an ideal are meant to be applied to all who follow Christ."[183]

The most important example of simplicity is that of the Holy Family. Jesus was born in a stable. A stable! The Son of God! Was that a fluke, or was there a message there, namely, as St. Francis understood, that *we* should live humbly, simply? Jesus lived simply, and encouraged His followers to do the same: "Blessed are you poor, for yours is the kingdom of God" (Luke 6:20).

If we read about the saints, we see that much of their credibility came from the fact that they lived in poverty. By their very lives they taught detachment from material goods and the importance of living for the Kingdom. This gives the gospel a richness that the world can admire. Even the media—yes the media!—could hardly resist little Mother Teresa of Calcutta, a poor sister who cared for the poor.

Jesus warned of the dangers of riches: "Woe to you that are rich, for you have received your consolation" (Luke 6:24); "It will be hard for a rich man to enter the kingdom of heaven" (Matt. 19:23).

[183] Thomas Dubay, *Happy Are You Poor*, 2nd ed., San Francisco: Ignatius Press, 2003, p. 13.

Why is the Lord so hard on the rich? St. Ignatius of Loyola wrote in the *Spiritual Exercises*:

> [The devil] bids [his demons] first to tempt men with the lust of riches ... that they may thereby more easily gain the empty honor of the world, and then come to unbounded pride. The first step in his snare is that of riches, the second honor, and the third, pride.[184]

Pride is the root of every vice.

Why is poverty so important? What does it accomplish? Living voluntary poverty is a profound sign to the world that we are living for a different world, a magnificent world to come.

Well, "I'm not really rich," some will say. "I live comfortably, but I'm not rich." But, those of us who live in the Western world today are some of the richest people who have ever lived.

St. Paul tells us there is great danger in riches:

> There is great gain in godliness with contentment; for we brought nothing into the world, and we cannot take anything out of the world; but if we have food and clothing, with these we shall be content. But those who desire to be rich fall into temptation, into a snare, into many senseless and hurtful desires that plunge men into ruin and destruction. For the love of money is the root of all evils; it is through this craving that some have wandered away from the faith. (1 Tim. 6:6–10)

James has strong words for the rich as well: "For the sun rises with its scorching heat and withers the grass; its flower falls, and its beauty perishes. So will the rich man fade away in the midst of his pursuits." (James 1:11).

[184] St. Ignatius of Loyola, *Spiritual Exercises*, Garden City, NY: Doubleday, 1964, p. 76.

THE POOR

There is another reason not to be rich: we are responsible for the poor. We cannot live in relative luxury while the poor do not have enough to eat: Jesus said, "As you did it to one of the least of these my brethren, you did it to me" (Matt. 25:40).

TITHING

How much should we give? The answer, as we saw earlier, is broadly given in Scripture. In the Old Testament it is recommended that we give one-tenth of our income back to the Lord (Deut. 15:28–29; Num. 18:23–34). Some suggest that we give 5 percent to the poor and 5 percent to support the Church.

Pope John Paul II pointed out, "Children must grow up with a correct attitude of freedom with regard to material goods, by adopting a simple and austere lifestyle and being fully convinced that 'man is more precious for what he is than for what he has.' "[185] Parents who buy their children expensive sneakers, chains, leather jackets, or give them expensive gifts for birthdays or Christmas are not teaching them a "simple and austere lifestyle."

Living simply would preclude expensive visits to the beauty parlor or upscale barber shop as well. Much of what costs dearly to have done by a professional can be accomplished for a fraction of the amount at home.

If you want to live simply for Christ, you should:

a) live well within your means (meaning buying a house and car you can *easily* afford);

b) avoid pouring money down the drain by keeping a credit card debt;

[185] Pope John Paul II, *Familiaris Consortio*, n. 37.

c) keep your house and car in good repair; and

d) shrink your appetite for buying.

If you do these things, you'll be living simply, and you'll always have enough.

Your standard of living should be based not so much on your income but on your faith commitment. Stoic philosopher Epictetus said, "Wealth consists not in having great possessions, but in having few wants."

21

FRUITS OF THE HOLY SPIRIT

MANY YEARS AGO, a young man came to see me, having just returned to the Church about six months before. He told me he had some Catholic friends who seemed to have a very strong faith and were consistently loving. "How can I get that kind of faith, and love?"

I told him that faith, firm faith, as St. Thomas Aquinas calls it, is a fruit of the Holy Spirit, as is love, or charity. I explained, "The fruits are the last thing to appear on a tree, so it will take you time to develop these as you grow in the spiritual life. It may take years but it's worth it." According to the *Catechism*,

> The *fruits* of the Spirit are perfections that the Holy Spirit forms in us as the first fruits of eternal glory. The tradition of the Church lists twelve of them: "charity, joy, peace, patience, kindness, goodness, generosity, gentleness, faithfulness, modesty, self-control, chastity." (CCC 1832)

PATIENCE

The fruits of the Holy Spirit are a kind of barometer to indicate how we are doing in our spiritual journey. For example, patience: if we are able to wait patiently for things to happen, this is a sign of spiritual advancement. Perhaps the acid test of patience is when we are behind the wheel of a car, and the person ahead is inexplicably crawling along.

KINDNESS

A well-known moral theologian shared the advice he received from his father on his wedding day. His father called him aside and told him to remember one word in his marriage: kindness. He thought little of it at the time, but as his marriage progressed, he saw more and more that it was great advice. How many marriages could be saved if both parties were consistently kind.

How pleasant it is when a person greets strangers with a smile. There are many people walking around in our world who are hurting a great deal inside for various reasons. What a boost it can be for one of them to receive a warm greeting from a stranger. Christians should be in the habit of giving such a greeting. We can make a habit out of kindness so we can express it naturally.

Perhaps the greatest challenge is showing kindness to our enemies, or to those who have hurt us. St. Thérèse of Lisieux lived with a nun who always rubbed her the wrong way. Whenever she saw her, she would smile, pray for her, and offer God all her virtues and merits. She showed her every kindness whenever she could. One day, the sister asked, "Sister Thérèse, will you please tell me what attracts you so much to me. You give me such a charming smile whenever we meet." Thérèse answered that it was because she was "happy to see her." She was indeed happy: happy to love someone she didn't like.[186]

---

[186] St. Thérèse of Lisieux, *The Autobiography of St. Thérèse of Lisieux: The Story of a Soul*, trans. by John Beevers, pp. 126, 127; and St. Thérèse of Lisieux, *Story of A Soul: The Autobiography of St. Thérèse of Lisieux*, trans. by John Clarke, p. 223.

One person went to visit a relative who could be quite difficult at times. When things started out badly she prayed to St. Thérèse to help her be kind to the relative. The next morning the relative became quite pleasant!

It is most important for parents to be kind to their children. They should discipline them fairly, but even in meting out punishment, they should try to be kind. Teenagers often can deal with the punishment they receive from their parents, but not the silent treatment they may receive from them for a week or two. One mother complained that her son's grandmother would go to her son's room and console him when he was sent there for punishment. When she asked her priest what she should do about it, he replied, "Wait 'til she is finished, and then go up and console him yourself."

Sarcasm is a vice opposed to kindness since it is caustic witticism. There is always a bite to sarcasm. Facetiousness, on the other hand, is a harmless witticism, a humorous quip about the ironies of life. To live out the virtue of kindness, we should eliminate all sarcasm. Another destroyer of kindness is bad moods. When we give in to a mood we are saying to everyone in our presence, in effect, "How I feel is more important than you or your comfort." The people who are cheerful almost all the time are not ordinarily mood-free; they just refuse to give in to their moods. Everyone has moods, and, as something not willed, there is nothing wrong with them. But, it is what we do with them that determines whether or not we are virtuous, living in the Spirit.

Many presume that there are just some people who are cheerful all the time, and some who are not, and that's the way it will continue to be. Not so. A number of people have exercised their will to change and become cheerful. This was the case with St. Thérèse of Lisieux, who was melancholy as a child, but through great effort (and grace) she became a bubbling sanguine personality whom all the sisters in her convent wanted to spend time with.

One of the ways I have seen people overcome their melancholy and negative personality is to begin to praise God for everything that happens in their life, good or bad. This is based in part on Romans 8:28: "We know that all things work out onto good for those who love God."[187] Those who love God and believe that wholeheartedly can trust that, no matter what happens, good will come of it.[188] It is also based on the fact that by embracing crosses, we can save souls (more on this in the next chapter). I have observed many people change from being rather negative to becoming quite positive simply by making a habit of praising God in every situation.

Some claim shyness as their reason to not give a warm facade in public. It seems, however, that many people are shy until they work at overcoming it. And, even shy people should be able to offer a warm smile to those they meet. Those who make a habit of that are living out the virtue of kindness and practicing Christian love.

Courtesy is another part of kindness. We read in Sacred Scripture, "Remind [the people] to be submissive to rulers and authorities, to be obedient, to be ready for any honest work, to speak evil of no one, to avoid quarreling, to be gentle, and to show perfect courtesy toward all men" (Titus 3:1–2). St. Francis of Assisi said, "Courtesy is one of the properties of God, who of His courtesy, gives His sun and rain to the just and the unjust: and courtesy is the sister of charity by which hatred is extinguished and love is cherished."[189]

---

[187] Translation is the author's.

[188] One of the key promoters of this custom is a Methodist minister, Merlin Carothers, in his "praise books," especially his first book, *Prison to Praise*, (Escondido, CA: Merlin Carothers, 1970 — eighteen million in print!) in which he describes the many miracles which occurred for those who trusted enough to praise God always.

[189] Found in Fr. Cuthbert, O.S.F.C., *Life of St. Francis of Assisi*, London: Longmans, Green and Co., 1921, p. 180.

There are many books written on courtesy. One I would recommend is *A Book of Courtesy*, some key points of which follow:

- Be on time (habitual lateness is often a sign of pride).
- Make a habit of saying please and thank you to *everyone*, regardless of age or social status.
- Don't interrupt and don't contradict (e.g., "No it isn't.").
- Return calls or emails within a day; answer invitations within a week if possible.
- If you are going to be late, call and let the host know.
- If you miss an appointment, call and apologize strongly and humbly.
- Turn cell phones off when with others or in a meeting or in church. If you must take a call, go somewhere private. Avoid being glued to a cell phone when with others.[190]

We all could probably find something on this list we need to work on. It is said that good manners are a series of inconveniences to make others feel comfortable.

GENTLENESS

Gentleness is opposed to anger, which poisons so many relationships—especially marriages. Granted, there is such a thing as just anger. St. Thomas Aquinas wrote, "If one is angry in accordance with right reason, one's anger is deserving of praise."[191] However, anger is numbered among the seven cardinal sins. Thus, it is ordinarily one of the "hinge" or root sins.

We read in James:

---

[190] Some of these points are drawn from Sr. Mary Mercedes, O.P., *A Book of Courtesy: The Art of Living with Yourself and Others*, San Francisco: HarperCollins, 2001.

[191] St. Thomas Aquinas, *Summa Theologica*, II–II q158, Benziger Brothers, vol II, 1948, p. 1838.

> Let every man be quick to hear, slow to speak, slow to anger, for the anger of man does not work the righteousness of God. Therefore put away all filthiness and rank growth of wickedness and receive with meekness the implanted word, which is able to save your souls.... If any one thinks he is religious, and does not bridle his tongue but deceives his heart, this man's religion is vain. (James 1:19–21, 26)

The feeling of anger is not, of course, a sin, since feelings may come over us without our willing them. But, the one who cultivates the feeling of anger, or acts on such a feeling in an unreasonable way, is guilty of sin. Anger often stems from pride.[192] Thus, to overcome anger we should pray for the virtue of humility.

Gentleness and kindness would, it seems, preclude foul language or cursing. The mouth that receives the Lord in Holy Communion should not be uttering obscenities. The measure of morality, as Pope John Paul II said in *Veritatis splendor*, is Jesus Himself. I doubt Jesus ever said a foul word.

FAITHFULNESS

Faithfulness (*pistis* in Greek) is more than faith. It is a firm belief in Christ which is lived out, especially by acts of love. We might apply St. Paul's expression, "faith working through love" (Gal. 5:6) here. It involves a lived-out commitment to Christ, and it implies trust and obedience. This fruit is a faithfulness that is strong, based on years of prayer and practicing the Faith. Prayer, the sacraments and Mass, and reading the saints seem to be the best ways to deepen our faithfulness.

---

[192] This author has written a short book on anger, *Overcoming Sinful Anger*, Nashua, NH: Sophia Institute Press, 2015.

CHARITY (LOVE)

This fruit is the Greek word *agape*, something we considered earlier. It is a supernatural active concern for the good of all, including our enemies, or for serving God in all things. Like faithfulness, as a fruit of the Holy Spirit, it is a firm habit, and quick to be exercised.

GOODNESS

Goodness refers to doing what is good and right, that is, being a moral person. In the Kingdom goodness and beauty are one. On earth there is no necessary connection between goodness and beauty. There are many beautiful people who are not good, and there are many good people who are not beautiful. But in the life to come they are one. The ugliness of those who lived evil lives on earth will be clearly seen by all. The inner beauty of those who were good will shine for all to see. The deeper our goodness and holiness in this life, the more beautiful we will be in the next.

JOY

This fruit is the spiritual joy that comes from a strong relationship with God. St. Bonaventure said, "A spiritual joy is the greatest sign of divine grace dwelling in a soul."[193] And, St. Francis of Assisi said, "Spiritual joy is as necessary to the soul as blood is to the body."[194] Jesus told the disciples:

> As the Father has loved me, so have I loved you; abide in my love. If you keep my commandments, you will abide in my love, just as I have kept my Father's commandments and abide

---

[193] St. Bonaventure, found in Alban Butler, *The Lives of the Fathers, Martyrs, and Other Principal Saints*, vol. 7, J. Duffy, 1866, p. 146.
[194] Omer Englebert, *St. Francis of Assisi: A Biography*, Ann Arbor, MI: Servant Books, 1979, p. 84.

in his love. These things I have spoken to you, that my joy may be in you, and that your joy may be full. (John 15:9–11).

Can we find joy only in God? Spiritual joy, yes. There are other kinds of joy which stem from our interaction with the world, and these can be good. However, As Cardinal Newman wrote, "The true Christian rejoices in those earthly things which give joy, but in such a way as not to care for them when they go."[195] As Christians, we are to find joy in all things — including suffering. St. Clare said, "Melancholy is the poison of devotion. When one is in tribulation, it is necessary to be more happy and more joyful because one is nearer to God."[196]

The Christian does not wait for a good feeling to be spiritually joyful. St. John Vianney said, "It is always springtime in the heart that loves God."[197] Merlin Carothers, one of the foremost proponents of praising and thanking God in all things, wrote,

> Accepting every little thing that happens with joy and thanksgiving will release the power of God in and through us, and we will soon experience a feeling of joy as well. But don't look for the feeling as a sign. Our praise and thanksgiving must be based on faith in God's word, not on our feelings.[198]

If we are to have the fruits of the Spirit, we must live by the Spirit and not by feelings. According to Cardinal Newman, "We must live in sunshine, even when we sorrow."[199]

---

[195] St. John Henry Newman, *Parochial Sermons*, vol. I, New York: D. Appleton and Co., 1843, p. 194.

[196] Jill Haak Adels, *The Wisdom of the Saints: An Anthology*, p. 193.

[197] Ibid.

[198] Merlin Carothers, *Power in Praise*, Escondido, CA: Carothers, 1972, p. 104.

[199] St. John Henry Newman, *Parochial Sermons*, vol. V, London: Rivington, 1840, p. 307.

How important it is to cultivate joy! St. Thomas Aquinas wrote, "No one can live without delight and that is why a man deprived of spiritual joy goes over to carnal pleasures."[200] So, "Rejoice in the Lord always; again I will say, Rejoice" (Phil. 4:4).

PEACE

When Jesus rose from the dead, He appeared to His disciples and greeted them, "Peace be with you" (John 20:19). He repeated this on that visit, and then again when He came a week later. He told them to wish peace on the house of those with whom they stayed, and "if the house is worthy, let your peace come upon it; but if it is not worthy, let your peace return to you" (Matt. 10:13). And, He told His disciples He was giving them a new kind of peace: "My peace I give to you; not as the world gives do I give to you" (Jn 14:27).

The supernatural peace that Christ gives is the result of trust. And trust, in turn, is the result of drawing close to God through spiritual activities. We will consider trust more in the next chapter.

One thing that kills peace is resentment. How many go around with residual anger because they hang on to resentment about what their husband or wife did, or what their sister or their boss did? But if we bear injustices patiently and forgive all injuries (two of the spiritual works of mercy), resentment flies away and our peace returns. If we feel resentful, we should either try to resolve it by gently asking for better behavior or by embracing the injustice as a penance.

It seems that many people are constantly in turmoil. They cannot find peace because they are concerned about all sorts of things rather than choosing the better part, focusing on Christ (Luke 10:42). So often we forget to live out the Serenity Prayer: "God, give us grace to accept

---

[200] Found in Jill Haak Adels, *The Wisdom of the Saints: An Anthology*, p. 191.

with serenity the things that cannot be changed, courage to change the things which should be changed, and the wisdom to distinguish the one from the other." There is more to this prayer, by Reinhold Niebuhr:

> Living one day at a time,
> Enjoying one moment at a time,
> Accepting hardship as a pathway to peace,
> Taking, as Jesus did,
> This sinful world as it is,
> Not as I would have it,
> Trusting that You will make all things right,
> If I surrender to Your will,
> So that I may be reasonably happy in this life,
> And supremely happy with You forever in the next.[201]

True, lasting, supernatural peace comes from God alone. Right after St. Paul urges the Philippians to rejoice always, to show others their kindness, to get rid of anxiety, and to pray to God while thanking Him, he tells them, "And the peace of God, which passes all understanding, will keep your hearts and your minds in Christ Jesus" (Phil. 4:7). St. Augustine believed that the very essence of Heaven would be peace, and he urged us to seek that peace here as well because, as he put it, "You have made us for yourself, and our heart is restless until it rests in you."[202]

GENEROSITY

All the saints were deeply generous. When they erred, they almost always erred on the side of generosity. This was the case of St. Bernard,

---

[201] The prayer as we have quoted it is different from the popularized one but appears to be the original.

[202] St. Augustine of Hippo, *The Confessions of Saint Augustine*, p. 43.

St. John Vianney, and others who fasted too severely at first and then had to learn to moderate their fasting by prudence. The woman who anointed Jesus with expensive perfumed oil did not pour it out drop by drop, but broke the jar, thereby insuring that she had to pour it *all* on Jesus (Mark 14:3). We should pray for such generosity, giving to the Lord and His people without counting the cost. Our prayer should be that of St. Ignatius of Loyola who wrote this Prayer for Generosity:

> Dearest Lord, teach me to be generous.
> Teach me to serve You as You deserve
> To give and not to count the cost
> To fight and not to heed the wounds
> To toil and not to seek for rest
> To labor and not ask for any reward,
> Except that of knowing that I am doing Your will.[203]

SELF-CONTROL

Self-control, as mentioned earlier under temperance, is extremely important for the Christian, especially in living a moral life. Pope John Paul II and Plato called this self-mastery, that is, the ability to control your actions by reason. When it comes to the appetites, self-control is not a full virtue. A virtue enables us to do good *joyfully, easily, and promptly*, as Aristotle taught. However, while a person is working to train the appetites (for sex, food, drink, and any other pleasurable thing), self-control is essential to control our behavior until the appetites are trained.

[203] St. Ignatius, adapted by G. P. Geoghegan, *A Collection of My Favorite Prayers*, Lulu.com, 2006, p. 91.

CHASTITY

We discussed the virtue of chastity under temperance earlier. Real chastity, that is, peace about refraining from illicit sexual activity, is a key indicator of spiritual maturity.

MODESTY

As we discussed earlier, modesty in dress serves chastity, especially in women. When a woman dresses modestly and with class, she is far more likely to be treated as a person, as someone with dignity. When she dresses immodestly, she is more likely to be viewed and treated as an object of enjoyment.

However, modesty has to do with more than just dressing. It is an essential part of humility, which is one of the most important virtues for a Christian. One who is modest does not parade his assets or accomplishments; a Christian realizes that any good that he has or good he has done is, in large part, a grace from God. Yes, he acknowledges what he has done well, or his gifts, but he doesn't seek notice or praise. His attitude is, "This is good, but, will it help me get to the Kingdom? If so, thanks be to God."

✠ ✠ ✠

The fruits of the Holy Spirit are barometers of our spiritual progress. As St. Paul wrote, "Those who belong to Christ Jesus have crucified the flesh with its passions and desires" (Gal. 5:24).

22

THE SHORTEST WAY TO THE KINGDOM

THERE ARE NO "shortcuts" to the Kingdom. The basics—prayer, the sacraments, Mass, and virtue—are essential, but there are certain elements of the spiritual life that make the journey to the Kingdom more efficient. The saints found them and have encouraged us to make use of them.

DEVOTION TO MARY

St. John Vianney seemed to know the whereabouts of souls who had died. The saint once told a widow whom he had never met and who had lost her husband to suicide,

> He is saved! He is in Purgatory.... Between the bridge and the water, he had time to make an act of contrition. Our Blessed Lady obtained that grace for him. Though he had no religion he sometimes prayed the Marian prayers with you in May. This merited him the grace of repentance.[204]

Mary is the kind of friend we want to have!

Apparently, the Lord loves us to pay attention to His Mother, and come to Him through her. Pope Pius XII once called devotion to Mary "a sign of 'predestination' according to the opinion of holy

---

[204] Adapted from Abbé Francis Trochu, *The Curé d'Ars: St. Jean-Marie Baptiste Vianney*, p. 540.

men."[205] In other words, this devotion is an indication that a person is on their way to the Kingdom.

St. Louis de Montfort, a great promoter of Marian devotion, suggested a long list of ways to live out this devotion. Here are a few:

- offering her works of praise, love and gratitude;
- calling on her with a joyful heart;
- doing things to please her;
- honoring her above all the other saints;
- meditating on her virtues, privileges, and actions;
- Praying the Rosary;
- wearing the scapular;
- singing hymns to her; and
- decorating her altars.[206]

And another, from Maximilian Kolbe and others — giving out Miraculous Medals.

There should be no question, based on the example of the saints, that devotion to Mary is the most efficient way to draw close to her Son. She brought Him forth to us. She is eager to bring us forth to Him.

DAILY MASS

There is nothing that brings us more grace than the Mass, and goodness knows we need all the grace we can get to enter the Kingdom. Perhaps this is why St. Joseph Cottelengo recommended daily Mass for everyone and said that those who do not go to daily Mass practice

---

[205] Pope Pius XII, *Mediator Dei* (On the Sacred Liturgy), November 20, 1947, n. 176, found at https://www.ewtn.com/catholicism/library/mediator-dei-21119.

[206] St. Louis de Montfort, *True Devotion to Mary*, n. 115, found in *God Alone: The Collected Writings of St. Louis Marie de Montfort*, pp. 324, 325.

bad time management. Pray, pray that God will give you the grace to go to Mass every day. God will answer that prayer.

INDULGENCES

Alas, the practice of receiving indulgences was much abused in the fifteenth century, but understood properly, this is a truly beneficial practice. The validity of indulgences was reiterated as a dogma at the Council of Trent; the scriptural basis cited for indulgences was Matthew 16:19 and John 20:23.[207]

As we saw in the chapter on loving our neighbors, we may help the dead a great deal by offering indulgences for them. We may also offer indulgences for ourselves. Either way, we gain much from attaining indulgences.

While attending Mass, we can receive a partial indulgence for listening attentively to the homily, and we can receive an indulgence each time we make the Sign of the Cross. We can receive a partial indulgence for humbly making a pious invocation (prayer) while carrying out our life's duties; by helping those in need by giving of ourselves or our goods; by abstaining from something good in a spirit of penance; or by giving witness to the faith to others.[208] And, of course, there are any number of prayers which gain a partial indulgence.[209]

PRAY THE ROSARY

Bishop Fulton Sheen wrote,

[207] Council of Trent, Session 25, December 4, 1563, Decree Concerning Indulgences, found at https://www.ewtn.com/catholicism/library/twentyfifth-session-of-the-council-of-trent-1492.

[208] Apostolic Penitentiary, *Manual of Indulgences*, pp. 25–36.

[209] For a list of works for plenary and partial indulgences, see Sacred Apostolic Penitentiary, *The Enchiridion of Indulgences*.

The Rosary is the meeting ground of the uneducated and
the learned; the place where simple love grows in knowledge
and where the knowing mind grows in love.... The rosary
is the book of the blind, where they see, and there enact
the greatest drama of love the world has ever known; it is
the book of the simple which initiates them into mysteries and knowledge more satisfying than the education of
other men; it is the book of the aged, whose eyes close on
the shadow of this world, and open on the substance of
the next. The power of the rosary is beyond description.[210]

There are fifteen promises that were made to Bl. Alan de la Roche
regarding those who pray the Rosary. They include the following:

I will deliver promptly from purgatory souls devoted to
my Rosary.
True children of my Rosary will enjoy great glory in heaven....
To those who propagate my Rosary I promise aid in all
their necessities....
Devotion to my Rosary is a special sign of predestination.[211]

The Rosary is so effective because it brings us through Mary to the
heart of Jesus. That's exactly where we want to end up.

HUMILITY

St. Augustine said, "If you ask me what is the most essential element in the teaching and morality of Jesus Christ, I would answer
you: the first is humility, the second is humility, and the third is

---

[210] Ven. Fulton J. Sheen, *The World's First Love*, New York: McGraw-
Hill, 1952, pp. 218, 219.

[211] "Our Lady's 15 Promises for Praying the Rosary," from Catholi-
cally, found at https://catholically.com/blogs/news/our-ladys-15-
promises-for-praying-the-rosary.

humility."[212] Shortly before St. Francis de Sales died, as he was leaving the Visitation sisters, Mother Superior asked him for one last piece of wisdom. He wrote three times on a piece of paper, "Humility."[213]

Humility is consistently praised in Sacred Scripture, and pride disdained: "He who is greatest among you shall be your servant; whoever exalts himself will be humbled, and whoever humbles himself will be exalted" (Matt. 23:11–12); and "He has scattered the proud in the imagination of their hearts, he has put down the mighty from their thrones, and exalted those of low degree" (Luke 1:51–52).

Humility is praised about twenty-five times in Scripture, the humble are praised about forty-eight times. Pride is held in contempt 103 times in Scripture, the proud are disdained about sixty-eight times. If there was ever a foundational virtue to strive for it is humility.

Cardinal Merry del Val (allegedly) wrote a litany of humility. What follows is an abbreviated and slightly altered version of that prayer:

> O Jesus! meek and humble of heart, make my heart like
>   unto thine.
> From the desire to be esteemed, deliver me.
> From the desire to be honored, deliver me.
> From the desire to be praised, deliver me.
> Teach me to accept humiliation, contempt,
>   rebukes, being slandered,
> being ignored, being insulted, being
>   wronged, and being belittled.
> Jesus, grant me the grace ...
> that others be admired more than I;

[212] St. Augustine, Letter 118, 22, found in "Humility, Source of Joy," from Opus Dei, found at http://www.opusdei.us/art.php?p=29262.

[213] Michael de la Bedoyere, *Francois de Sales*, [in print today under the title of *Saint Maker*, by Sophia Institute Press], New York: Harper & Brothers, 1960, p. 245.

that others be praised and I unnoticed;
that others be preferred to me in everything;
that others be holier than I, provided I
    become as holy as I should;
that I might imitate the patience and
    obedience of Your mother, Mary.
Amen.

Humility: don't leave home without it.

OBEDIENCE

We read in 1 Samuel: "Behold, to obey is better than sacrifice, and to hearken than the fat of rams" (1 Sam. 15:22). And, in Psalm 40, verse 8, "I delight to do thy will, O my God; thy law is within my heart."

St. Alphonsus Rodriguez wrote, "To pick up a [piece of] straw from the ground through obedience is more meritorious than to preach, to fast, to use the discipline to blood, and to make long prayers, of one's own will."[214] And St. Teresa of Ávila, when tempted to disobey her spiritual director and perform heroic acts of penance in imitation of a holy woman of the town, was told by our Lord, "Do you look at the penance she does? I put higher value on your obedience."[215]

The Lord appeared to St. Margaret Mary Alacoque once and said:

> I am the absolute Master of My gifts, as also of My creatures, and nothing will be able to prevent Me from carrying out My designs. Therefore, not only do I desire that you should do what your superiors command, but also that you should do nothing of all that I order you

---

[214] "Obedience: A Bitter Gift," from American Institute of Health Care Professionals, found at https://aihcp.net/2012/08/24/obedience-a-bitter-gift/.

[215] Marcelle Auclair, *Teresa of Ávila*, p. 363.

without their consent. I love obedience, and without it, no one can please Me.[216]

St. Thérèse of Lisieux performed few great penances, but she obeyed just about everyone, including those who had no authority over her. St. Francis of Assisi strove for a similar obedience.

Once when Teresa of Ávila was trying to figure out whether to found her next convent in Madrid or Seville, her spiritual director told her to ask the Lord in prayer. The Lord told her to go to Madrid. When she spoke to her director again, he ordered her to go to Seville. She obeyed her director. He later discovered what the Lord had said to her and asked why she obeyed him rather than the Lord. She answered, "Faith tells me what you commanded is the will of God, but I have no assurance that revelations are." Sometime later, the Lord appeared to her and told her she had done the right thing, so much did He value obedience to her superiors. He told her He now wanted her to go to Seville.[217]

St. Philip Neri said, "A soul possessed of this spirit of obedience cannot be lost: a soul devoid of this spirit cannot be saved."[218] Jesus Himself said to St. Maria Faustina, "You give me greater glory by a single act of obedience than by long prayers and mortification."[219]

We should note that obedience, even for a religious who has vowed obedience, does not apply to an immoral command. Our first obedience must be to God and what is moral.

---

[216] St. Margaret Mary Alacoque, *The Autobiography of Saint Margaret Mary*, pp. 61, 62.

[217] William Thomas Walsh, *St. Teresa of Ávila*, Rockford, IL: TAN Books, 1993, pp. 446, 447.

[218] Found in R. P. Quadrupani, *Light and Peace: Instructions for Devout Souls to Dispel Their Doubts and Allay Their Fears*, p. 1.

[219] Sr. Sophia Michalenko, *Mercy My Mission: Life of Sister Faustina H. Kowalska*, p. 137.

For the laity, obedience to liturgical norms, such as the proper way to receive Communion and obedience to traffic laws, would be examples of exercising this grace-giving virtue.[220] We must also be obedient to our duties in life. Some examples of this might include schoolwork for a student, care of children for a parent, doing one's work for an employee. It is a virtue to do the things we are obliged to do before doing the things we'd like to do.

MERCY: GIVE IT AND SEEK IT

Our Blessed Lord appeared to St. Maria Faustina, an obscure nun in Poland, from 1931 to 1938, to announce that mercy was God's greatest attribute and to have her spread a new devotion to His mercy. He showed her an image of Himself that He wanted painted and He promised that whoever venerated this image would not perish. The image depicted Jesus with two rays coming out of His heart, representing Blood and water that poured forth when His heart was pierced on Calvary. These two symbolize the Eucharist and Baptism. Jesus told her, "I desire that priests proclaim this great mercy of Mine toward souls of sinners . . . . I want to pour [the flames of mercy] out upon these souls."[221]

He told her we would not know peace until we place trust in His mercy. On September 13, 1935, Jesus gave her a new chaplet of prayers to pacify His anger: the Divine Mercy Chaplet. It consists of an Our Father, Hail Mary, and Apostles' Creed; then, using the rosary, on the Our Father beads, the prayer, *Eternal Father, I offer you the Body and Blood, soul and divinity of Your dearly beloved Son, our Lord Jesus Christ in atonement for our sins and those of the whole*

---

[220] Regarding the speed limit, most safe-driving advocates suggest staying within five miles per hour over the speed limit. It seems this is because officials keep the limits unduly low, knowing that drivers will exceed them by a certain amount no matter where they are set.

[221] Sr. Sophia Michalenko, *Mercy My Mission: Life of Sister Faustina H. Kowalska*, pp. 31, 32.

world. On the Hail Mary beads would come the prayer: *For the sake of His sorrowful Passion, have mercy on us and on the whole world.* Finally, would come three times the prayer, *Holy God, Holy Mighty One, Holy Immortal One, have mercy on us and on the whole world.*[222]

In November 1936, Jesus told Sr. Faustina that whoever would say the chaplet, especially just before death, would be received into His mercy. He promised he would defend them "as his own glory."[223]

He called for a Feast of Mercy on the Sunday after Easter, which Pope John Paul II instituted in 2000. Jesus promised that anyone who would confess and go to Communion on Mercy Sunday would receive a full remission of all punishment for sins.[224] It is said that Confession during Lent would fulfill the Confession condition.[225]

At another point, Jesus insisted that those who seek mercy should show it to others. This would include the works of mercy[226] and forgiveness, which Jesus said is essential if we wish to receive forgiveness (Matt. 6:14–15).

TRUST

When our Lord gave the image of Divine Mercy to Sr. Faustina, He indicated He wanted the caption at the bottom of the picture to read, "Jesus, I trust in you." He told her at one point:

[222] Sr. Sophia Michalenko, *Mercy My Mission: Life of Sister Faustina H. Kowalska*, p. 92.

[223] Sr. Sophia Michalenko, *Mercy My Mission: Life of Sister Faustina H. Kowalska*, pp. 120, 127. This differs from a plenary indulgence in that it is given directly by Christ, not through the Church.

[224] Sr. Sophia Michalenko, *Mercy My Mission: Life of Sister Faustina H. Kowalska*, p. 113.

[225] See "Frequently Asked Questions," from The Divine Mercy, found at https://www.thedivinemercy.org/library/faq-common.

[226] St. Maria Faustina, *Divine Mercy in My Soul: Diary of Saint Maria Faustina Kowalska*, n. 742, pp. 297, 298.

Encourage souls to place great trust in my fathomless mercy. Let the weak, sinful soul have no fear to approach me, for even if it had more sins than there are grains of sand in the world, all will be drowned in the immeasurable depths of my mercy.[227]

He also told her:

The graces of my mercy are drawn by means of one vessel only, and that is trust. The more a soul trusts, the more it will receive. Souls that trust boundlessly are a great comfort to me, because I pour all the treasures of my grace into them.[228]

Jesus further told her regarding Confession:

Tell souls that from this fount of mercy souls draw graces solely with the vessel of trust. If their trust is great, there is no limit to my generosity. The torrents of grace inundate humble souls.[229]

Pray, pray much, for the virtue of trust.

THE CROSS

Bearing a cross for the Lord is not an option for the Christian. Jesus said, "If any man would come after me, let him deny himself and take up his cross and follow me. For whoever would save his life will lose it, and whoever loses his life for my sake will find it" (Matt. 16:24–25). The cross is a necessary condition to follow Christ, and, paradoxically, those who are willing to lose all for Christ will gain happiness; those who try to find happiness by avoiding suffering will never find it.

---

[227] Sr. Sophia Michalenko, *Mercy My Mission: Life of Sister Faustina H. Kowalska*, p. 152.

[228] Sr. Sophia Michalenko, *Mercy My Mission: Life of Sister Faustina H. Kowalska*, p. 215.

[229] Sr. Sophia Michalenko, *Mercy My Mission: Life of Sister Faustina H. Kowalska*, p. 218.

Jesus emphasized the importance of the cross when Peter tried to dissuade Him from it. He told him "Get behind me, Satan!" (Matt. 16:23). Satan! Satan is the enemy of the cross. Bishop Sheen elaborated, "When the devil is stripped of all his trappings, the ultimate goal of the demonic is to avoid the Cross, mortification, self-discipline and self-denial."[230] Jesus told St. Rose of Lima once, "Without the cross [souls] can find no road to climb to heaven."[231]

Should we ask for suffering? An article appeared in a Catholic magazine some years ago suggesting we should *not* ask for suffering. Alas, the author failed to consider the very prayer of the Church. For example, in the intercessions for Morning Prayer, Easter Sunday: "Lord, you walked the way of suffering and crucifixion; may we suffer and die with you and rise again to share your glory." And, in the opening prayer for the Mass of St. Philip the Apostle (May 3) we find:

> God our Father, every year you give us joy on the festival of the Apostles Philip and James. By the help of their prayers may we share in the suffering, death and resurrection of your Son and come to the eternal vision of your glory.[232]

Lex orandi, lex credendi—the norm of prayer is the norm of belief.

Some are reluctant to pray for suffering, but I believe that by asking for the "suffering, grace, and humility to become a saint," we are likely to suffer less and more sweetly than if we did not pray for it.

---

[230] Ven. Fulton J. Sheen, *Treasure in Clay: The Autobiography of Fulton J. Sheen*, p. 334. (Now published by Ignatius Press.)

[231] "Unfathomable Treasure of Grace—Rose of Lima," from Crossroads Initiative, found at https://www.crossroadsinitiative.com/media/articles/rose-lima-grace-august-23/.

[232] There are other examples, such as a) the closing prayer for the Mass of the Holy Rosary (October 7), b) Evening Prayer, Friday, Week 3, closing prayer, and c) Morning Prayer, Second Wednesday of Lent, final intercession.

St. John Vianney said, "He who goes to meet the cross is in fact avoiding crosses."[233] And, another John — St. John of the Cross — wrote, "He who seeks not the cross of Christ seeks not the glory of Christ."

Pope Benedict XVI explained how to deal with suffering:

> It is when we attempt to avoid suffering by withdrawing from anything that might involve hurt, when we try to spare ourselves the effort and pain of pursuing truth, love, and goodness, that we drift into a life of emptiness, in which there may be almost no pain, but the dark sensation of meaninglessness and abandonment is all the greater. It is not by sidestepping or fleeing from suffering that we are healed, but rather by our capacity for accepting it, maturing through it and finding meaning through union with Christ, who suffered with infinite love.[234]

St. Francis de Sales wrote:

> The everlasting God has in his wisdom foreseen from eternity the cross He now presents to you as a gift from His inmost Heart. This cross He now sends you He has considered with His all-knowing eyes, understood with His divine mind, tested with His wise justice, warmed with loving arms and weighed with His own hands to see that it be not one inch too long and not one ounce too heavy for you. He has blessed it with His Holy Name, anointed it with His consolation, taken one last glance at you and your courage, and then sent it to you from

---

[233] Alfred Monnin, *The Curé of Ars*, trans. by Bertram Wolferstam, S.J., St. Louis, MO: Herder Book Co., 1924, p. 165.
[234] Pope Benedict XVI, *Spe salvi*, n. 37.

heaven, a special greeting from God to you, an alms of the All-Merciful Love of God.[235]

What does it mean to "carry our cross"? It means to embrace every trial, every setback, every illness or injury, every bit of suffering we face for love of God and for the remission of sins. It also means fasting and doing penance in accord with reason (but never *beyond* reason!).

Which is more beneficial, to choose our penances, or to accept what God sends us? Although we should do both, St. Francis de Sales preferred

chance mortifications, however small, which came unsought, to bigger things done by personal choice.... He used to say, "Where there is less of our own choice there is more of God." Some of the chance mortifications he accepted willingly were, when people stopped him from getting on with some urgent business, when he met with opposition, [or] came across difficult people. And, he never complained.[236]

In the Letter to the Philippians, we are told of those who lived for this world, and had no use for the cross:

For many, of whom I have often told you and now tell you weeping as well, go around in a way which reveals them to be enemies of the cross of Christ. They will end in disaster! Their God is their belly; their glory is in their shame. They are set upon worldly things. But our citizenship is in heaven. (Phil. 3:18–20)[237]

---

[235] "St. Francis de Sales on the Gift of the Cross in Our Lives," from The Fathers of Mercy, found at https://fathersofmercy.com/st-francis-de-sales-gift-cross-lives/.

[236] St. Jane de Chantal, *St. Francis de Sales: A Testimony by St. Chantal*, trans. by Elisabeth Stopp, London: Faber and Faber, 1967, p. 81.

[237] The translation is the author's.

DEVOTION TO THE ANGELS

It seems that the more we call on our guardian angel, the more aid we receive. After seldom praying to my angel for several years, I read the following story. A young woman was returning to her home in Brooklyn and as she neared her destination, she saw a menacing man leaning against a building. She prayed, "Guardian Angel, protect me." and walked by the man calmly. When she got out of sight, she ran the rest of the way and once inside her apartment, she immediately locked the door. The next day she heard from a neighbor that a rape had occurred in the very place where she saw the man, and at the very time she had passed by. So she offered to describe the man to the police, since she was sure he was the one. They had already arrested someone, but they invited her down to pick him out of a lineup. She did, and then she asked one of the officers why the man hadn't gone after her. The officer wondered too, so he described her to the assailant and asked why he did nothing to her. His reply: "I remember her. But, why would I attack her? She was walking down the street with two big guys, one on either side."[238]

This and other stories convinced me I had paid too little attention to my angel. Since reading them I have called on him often, and I believe I've gotten more protection as a result.

A number of saints had great devotion to their guardian angels, including St. Francis de Sales, St. Bernard, St. Rose of Lima, and St. Jerome. God has given us each a heavenly protector. We should make use of that gift daily.

PERSEVERE

It may not qualify as a short way to the Kingdom, but it is a sure way: perseverance. Resolve never to give up praying and striving

---

[238] Joan Wester Anderson, *Where Angels Walk*, New York: Ballantine Books, 1993, pp. 93–95.

for virtue, no matter how many times you fall. Jesus promised us success:

> I tell you, Ask, and it will be given you; seek, and you will find; knock, and it will be opened to you. For every one who asks receives, and he who seeks finds, and to him who knocks it will be opened." (Luke 11:9–10)

23

SUMMARY

Many today underestimate the tremendous happiness of Heaven, and the grace-empowered effort it will take to get there. We also tend to forget the horror of Hell and the great suffering of Purgatory for those who do not take seriously the universal call to holiness.[239] Thinking often of these things should strongly motivate us to pursue true holiness.

The way to holiness is straightforward: pursue the life of grace and seek to become a new creation in Christ by living the virtues. Through prayer, the sacraments, the Mass, and reading the saints we can know and begin on the path to holiness and stay motivated. Through striving for virtue, practicing the spiritual and corporal works of mercy, and cultivating the fruits of the Holy Spirit, we can become the saints God intended us to be. As the saints knew well, holiness is the shortest way to the Kingdom, and the happiest way to live.

✠ ✠ ✠

May the God of peace himself make you completely holy
and may you be kept entirely blameless
—spirit, soul, and body—
for the coming of our Lord Jesus Christ.
The one who calls you is faithful,
and he will do it. (1 Thess. 5:23, 24)[240]

---

[239] Vatican II, Lumen Gentium, n. 40.
[240] The translation is the author's.

Sophia Institute

Sophia Institute is a nonprofit institution that seeks to nurture the spiritual, moral, and cultural life of souls and to spread the gospel of Christ in conformity with the authentic teachings of the Roman Catholic Church.

Sophia Institute Press fulfills this mission by offering translations, reprints, and new publications that afford readers a rich source of the enduring wisdom of mankind.

Sophia Institute also operates the popular online resource CatholicExchange.com. *Catholic Exchange* provides world news from a Catholic perspective as well as daily devotionals and articles that will help readers to grow in holiness and live a life consistent with the teachings of the Church.

In 2013, Sophia Institute launched Sophia Institute for Teachers to renew and rebuild Catholic culture through service to Catholic education. With the goal of nurturing the spiritual, moral, and cultural life of souls, and an abiding respect for the role and work of teachers, we strive to provide materials and programs that are at once enlightening to the mind and ennobling to the heart; faithful and complete, as well as useful and practical.

Sophia Institute gratefully recognizes the Solidarity Association for preserving and encouraging the growth of our apostolate over the course of many years. Without their generous and timely support, this book would not be in your hands.

www.SophiaInstitute.com
www.CatholicExchange.com
www.SophiaInstituteforTeachers.org

Sophia Institute Press is a registered trademark of Sophia Institute.
Sophia Institute is a tax-exempt institution as defined by the
Internal Revenue Code, Section 501(c)(3). Tax ID 22-2548708.